MARTIN BUBER
(1878–1965)

Martin Buber's Ontology

Northwestern University
STUDIES IN *Phenomenology &*
Existential Philosophy

Robert E. Wood

Martin Buber's Ontology

An Analysis of
I AND THOU

NORTHWESTERN UNIVERSITY PRESS

EVANSTON   1969

Robert E. Wood is Associate Professor of Philosophy
at St. Joseph's College, Rensselaer, Indiana.

To Marjorie, Robert, Gregory, Mary, David, and Mark for the lines of relation which meet in the eternal thou

Contents

Preface

AROUND THE TURN OF THE CENTURY two of the major problems confronting philosophic thought were the impasse between subjectivity and objectivity and the tension between spirit and life. Edmund Husserl, for example, saw the major problem to be the deadlock between an objectivity which tended to swallow up all subjectivity in naïve naturalism and a subjectivity which tended to reduce all objectivity to a function of the *cogito*.[1] The second problem, that of the relation between spirit and life, between the spontaneous immediacy of life and the detached and deliberative character of spirit, is identified by Ernst Cassirer as the central problem of thought in recent times.[2]

At the turn of the century Martin Buber arrived on the philosophic scene and confronted these problems from within the perspective of his own personal preoccupations. The path to his maturity was one long struggle with the problem of unity—in particular with the problem of the unity of spirit and life; and he saw the problem itself to be rooted in the supposition of the primacy of the subject-object relation, with subjects "over here," objects "over there," and their relation a matter of subjects "taking in" objects or, alternatively, constituting them. But Buber moved into a position which undercuts the subject-object dichot-

1. Edmund Husserl, "The Crisis of European Humanity and Philosophy," *The Search for Being*, ed. and trans. Jean Wilde and William Kimmel (New York: Noonday, 1962), pp. 378–413.
2. Ernst Cassirer, " 'Spirit' and 'Life' in Contemporary Philosophy," *The Philosophy of Ernst Cassirer*, The Library of Living Philosophers, ed. Paul Schilpp (Menasha, Wis.: Banta, 1949), p. 858.

omy and initiates a second "Copernican revolution" in philosophical thought.[3] Kant had formulated the first such revolution; instead of subjects moving about objects, Kant saw the opposite: the objective world as a function of cognitive subjectivity.[4] While steadfastly holding to the Kantian position as valid on its own level,[5] Martin Buber introduced the notion of an ontologically prior relation of *Presence*, binding subject and object together in an identity-in-difference which he termed the I-Thou relation and which constitutes the region of what he calls the Between (*das Zwischen*). The spirit-and-life problem stems from the exaltation of subject-object; I-Thou binds together spirit and life through the introduction of this new dimension of the Between. The present work is intended to carry out an examination of that new dimension as Buber presented it.

But the center of Buber's work is primarily descriptive, essentially intent upon bearing witness to an experience which he sees as central to human life. Toward the end of his long life, he admitted that he really had no "doctrine" in the sense of a sustained systematic treatment. He had simply pointed to certain connections between experiences. He described his function as leading men to the window, which he opened up so that they could see what is outside.[6] And from that descriptive center Buber's own way leads outward to the interpersonal applications of his experiences within the arena of practical life, where he came constantly to dwell. Hence he leaves to others the task of moving backwards into the ontological foundations and implications of his thought.[7] The present work, an explication of the ontological

3. Karl Heim, "Ontologie und Theologie," *Zeitschrift für Theologie und Kirche*, XI (1930), 333.

4. Immanuel Kant, *Critique of Pure Reason*, Preface to the Second Edition, B xvi–xvii.

5. IMB, p. 21. For a list of abbreviations used in these footnotes, see p. xv. Full publication data will be found in the Bibliography at the end of the book.

6. "Replies to My Critics," PMB, p. 693.

7. Emil Fackenheim, "Some Recent Works on and by Martin Buber," *Religious Education*, LIV (September–October, 1959), 416a. The term "ontological" is used here advisedly, in keeping with Buber's final usage, as against the term "metaphysical." In 1923, in "Von der Verseelung der Welt" (*Nachlese* [Heidelberg: Lambert Schneider, 1965], p. 149), he spoke of his *ontologism* as a synthesis between cosmologism and psychologism (or "materialism" and "idealism"). In 1938, in "What Is Man?" (WM, BMM, p. 122), he claimed it a

foundations of Martin Buber's thought, is intended as a contribution in this direction.

According to Buber's own statement, the work *I and Thou,* which appeared in 1923, gathers up all the preceding stages of his development and furnishes insights that were to be developed in his later works.[8] Hence it is methodologically convenient to focus attention upon *I and Thou* itself as the node of an analysis which will draw upon the total corpus of Buber's works. In addition to the value of this method in working out the ontological underpinnings, it becomes immediately evident from a perusal of the text itself that section-by-section clarification is in order.

The first chapter furnishes an introduction to the analysis proper, fitting *I and Thou* into the total context of Buber's life and thought. The second chapter deals with the general structure of *I and Thou,* in the sense of its stylistic form as well as its logical pattern. The next three chapters deal with the three parts of *I and Thou.*[9] A final chapter gathers up the results of the analysis in a summary of the ontological foundations of Martin Buber's thought.

I wish to thank the members of the college community at St. Joseph's in Rensselaer, Indiana, for supplying the conditions that made the writing of this work possible. I wish especially to

---

matter of necessity that every philosophic discipline "remain open and accessible, first to the ideas of metaphysics itself as the doctrine of being, of what is and of existence," though later in the same essay he criticized Scheler for letting his "consideration of the real man be permeated by a metaphysics" (p. 182). But near the end of his life, though he still spoke of his ontology, transcending psychologism and relativism ("Correspondence with Martin Buber," Robert C. Smith, correspondent, *Review of Existential Psychoanalysis and Psychiatry,* VI, No. 3 [1966], 248), he rejected any possession of, ability to provide, or even any *need for* a metaphysics on his part (IMB, p. 84)—which appears to reverse the 1938 position on the need for every philosophic discipline to remain open to metaphysics. Apparently the danger that metaphysics could poison the well of encounter led him to this reversal. See below, pp. 120 ff., for further discussion of metaphysics and ontology.

8. "Postscript," *I and Thou,* trans. Ronald G. Smith (New York: Scribner's, 1958), pp. 123–24.

9. The "Postscript" to this work will be treated merely as a contributory source, since it appeared much later than the original text (1957); it will therefore be assimilated into the body of the analysis of the three major parts of the book.

thank my students for their patience during the spring semester, 1967, when this work was being completed. Thanks are also due to Dr. Lottie Kendzierski for initially suggesting this work, to Dr. Beatrice Zedler for her critical comments, and to Mrs. Virginia Seidman for her careful work with the manuscript.

ROBERT E. WOOD

Rensselaer, Indiana
May, 1967

List of Abbreviations
of Buber's Works
Cited in Footnotes

Martin Buber's Ontology

1 / The Context

IN RELATION TO MARTIN BUBER's life and thought
and times *I and Thou* stands in much the same way as the
Republic in relation to Plato. Chronologically, the *Republic* (*ca.*
374 B.C.) stands just beyond the center of Plato's eighty-year
life (427–347 B.C.); *I and Thou* appeared in 1923, forty-five
years into a life that stretched from 1878 to 1965. Like the
Republic, *I and Thou* is rooted in an impulse toward developing the fullness of life, in whose service philosophy is seen to
stand,[1] and not in some purely curious, speculative interest.
Further, just as the *Republic* constitutes a watershed through
which all Plato's previous dialogues and out of which all his
future dialogues flow, so *I and Thou* gathers up the early stages
of Buber's thought and sets the tone for all that follows. Finally,
as the *Republic* witnesses to a revolution in thought, placing the
final object of knowing and aspiration beyond the impasses of
sensism, so, as we have already indicated, *I and Thou* constitutes
a revolution by opening up the sphere of the Between beyond the
impasses of subjectivism and objectivism with which modern
thought has been so mightily struggling.

In this chapter attention will be focused chiefly upon the
growth of Buber's thought up to *I and Thou* in 1923. The period
after 1923 will be considered mainly in terms of Buber's life,
since the content of the later writings will furnish the major part
of the material for our analysis of the text.

At the time of Buber's birth, Judaism was in a tremendous
state of ferment caused by the confluence of Hasidism and

1. Plato *Letter VII* 324B–326B.

[3]

Haskalah, of Jewish mystical piety and Jewish Enlightenment.[2] Buber's own thought was to emerge out of that ferment and terminate in the completed synthesis of these two streams.[3]

He was born in Vienna, February 8, 1878. Three years later, following the divorce of his parents, he moved to the home of his grandfather at Lemberg in Galicia. His grandfather, Solomon Buber, was a Midrash scholar and "one of the last great men of the Haskala," [4] and under his tutelage the young boy became immersed in Jewish culture. Both his grandparents stimulated his interest in the study of language, and he learned French, Hebrew, and Latin in addition to his native German and Polish. The unity underlying the multiplicity of languages became one of the earliest problems for the young boy [5] and expressed the *Urform* of what was to become his own life interest: unity and multiplicity.

From his ninth year he spent his summers with his father, whom he frequently accompanied to the Hasidic settlement in Sadagora in Bukovina. At the prayer house of the Hasidim he experienced what he considered the basic form of community rooted in common reverence and common joy.

But from his fourteenth year, as he left Solomon Buber's house to attend to his formal studies, the Enlightenment intellectualist strain took hold of him, alienated him from the piety of the Hasidim, and produced a state of uprootedness and restlessness that was to last to his twenty-sixth year. "From the heights of a rational man" he looked down upon the naïve piety of the Hasidim. He writes of his life with his grandfather:

> So long as I lived with him, my roots were firm, although many questions and doubts also jogged about in me. Soon after I left his house, the whirl of the age took me in. . . . My spirit was in steady and multiple movement, in an alternation of tension and release, determined by manifold influences, taking ever new shape, but without center and without growing substance.[6]

2. "Renaissance und Bewegung," JSJ, p. 272.
3. Hans Kohn, *Martin Buber, Sein Werk und seine Zeit,* 2d ed., revised by Robert Weltsch (Cologne: Melzer, 1961), p. 15.
4. *Ibid.,* p. 16.
5. *Begegnung, Autobiographische Fragmente* (Stuttgart: Kohlhammer, 1960), pp. 8–10.
6. "My Way to Hasidism," HMM, pp. 53–57.

A sensitive young man, at the age of fourteen Martin Buber responded strongly to the intellectual problems he began to confront. The eternal silence of infinite space which had terrified Pascal likewise gripped young Buber. The problems of space and time raised in him the questionableness of man's existence, a tiny being caught up in the hostile and indifferent universe. And the questions were raised, not merely in his intellect, but in his very being. His intellectual problems became problems of life, to such an extent that Buber was almost driven to suicide by the difficulty in coming to grips with space and time. At fifteen, however, he was saved from that alternative by a reading of Kant's *Prolegomena,* which demonstrated to his satisfaction that space and time belonged to the structure of the mind itself and that what really confronted him in the mysteries of space and time was thus the mystery of his own being.[7] The Kantian influence was to remain to the very end of his life.

In 1896, at the age of eighteen, Buber enrolled at the University of Vienna, where one of his teachers was F. Jodl, editor of the works of Ludwig Feuerbach. And it was Buber's reading of Feuerbach which gave a "decisive impetus" to the young man's thought.[8] That impetus was twofold. In the first place, Feuerbach placed philosophical anthropology, the question of man, at the center of the philosophic enterprise. In explicit opposition to Kant and Hegel, who focused upon human cognition as the center, Feuerbach centers upon man in his totality. In the second place, for Feuerbach, man himself is located, not in individuals, but in the relationship of man with man, in the I and the Thou.[9] It was Feuerbach who, for the first time, made the I-Thou relation the very center of his philosophizing.[10] This was to form the center of Buber's own thought: a philosophical anthropology whose locus is the Between. But at this early stage it remains an impetus, not yet the center. For, as the center, I-and-Thou appears only at the end of a process of development that passes through three stages, usually described as the mystical, the exis-

7. WM, BMM, pp. 134–37; *Begegnung,* pp. 16–17.
8. WM, BMM, p. 148.
9. Ludwig Feuerbach, *Grundsätze der Philosophie der Zukunft* (Leipzig, 1847), sec. 1, p. 1; sec. 37, pp. 62–63; secs. 61–65, pp. 83–84.
10. "Zur Geschichte des dialogischen Prinzips," W I, pp. 294–95.

tential, and the dialogical, in that order.[11] But the single thread that runs through the whole of Buber's life and thought, gathering them together into a dynamic unity, is his concern for unity: unity of the whole of Being, unity within an individual being, unity between individual beings. And the constant elements in that concern for unity were God, the world, and man, seen in varying relationships as his thought develops.

The first, the mystical, stage in that development was stimulated by his teachers at the University of Berlin, where he studied in the summer of 1898 and from the fall of 1899 to the summer of 1901. These teachers were Wilhelm Dilthey and Georg Simmel. Simmel's later work concentrated upon the role of religion in life, and especially upon the place of the mystics. His treatment of the correlation of Kantian thought with that of the speculative mysticism of Eckhart strikingly parallels Buber's own developing thought, in which Kant and the mystics are constantly present.[12] Dilthey was preoccupied with the unity of life which attained multiple expression in various types of world views.[13]

The relation between unity and multiplicity—specifically, the relation between the unity of God and the multiplicity of creatures—and the contribution to this problem made by the speculative mystics from Eckhart to Boehme were the topics of Buber's dissertation of 1900: *Beiträge zur Geschichte des Individuationsprinzips*. Buber chose this particular era in the history of thought because it was the era of transition from the transcendent God of the Middle Ages to the pantheistic God of the modern world. The latter notion was still running strong in the circles within which Buber moved at the universities of Berlin and Vienna.[14] In the dissertation he accepted the notion which

11. Maurice Friedman, *Martin Buber, The Life of Dialogue* (New York: Harper Torchbooks, 1955), p. 27. Henceforth this work will be referred to as Friedman, *Life*.

12. Georg Simmel, "The Fundamental Problems of Philosophy," *The Search for Being*, ed. and trans. Jean Wilde and William Kimmel (New York: Noonday, 1962), pp. 315–43.

13. Wilhelm Dilthey, *Dilthey's Philosophy of Existence*, trans. William Kluback and Martin Weinbaum (London: Vision Press, 1957), pp. 17–74.

14. Simon Maringer, *Martin Bubers Metaphysik der Dialogik in Zusammenhang neuerer philosophischer Strömungen* (Cologne: Steiner, 1936), pp. 15 ff.

Boehme took over from Valentine Weigel and which reached its full fruition in the work of Hegel: the notion that God becomes Himself through the development of the world.[15] In his later description of this period, Buber notes: "Since 1900 I had first been under the influence of German mysticism from Meister Eckhart to Angelus Silesius, according to which the primal ground of being, the nameless, impersonal Godhead, comes to 'birth' in the human soul." [16]

For Buber, however, there is always a mutual stimulation that occurs between the moment of speculation and the moment of life.[17] Later he described the life moment that speculation was meant to illuminate as the moment of the "religious," which lifted him out of the course of things, out of "the reliable permanence of appearances," "the context of life," shattering "first the firm world's structure, then the still firmer self-assurance," and delivering him over to fullness, "lighting a way into the lightning-piercing darkness of the mystery itself." [18] In attempting to clarify such a life moment, Buber immersed himself in the writings of speculative mysticism.

In the line of that orientation, he published his first important philosophic essay in 1901, "Ueber Jakob Boehme." Here he explained and apparently accepted the Renaissance notion of the microcosm, where God is present in His totality within each creature and comes to light in man. The cosmos itself is composed of two movements: the movement of conflict, through which individuals emerge as distinct, and the movement of love, which leads back to unity. The two movements complement each other; through conflict the Other is set over against us, and through love, which culminates in a world feeling, we unite with the Other—with the stone, the tree, the animal, and with our fellow men. And in this union of the I with the Thou, God comes to birth in the soul. Here Feuerbach is cited approvingly: "Man by himself is man in the ordinary sense of the term; man with

15. Franz Rosenzweig, "Zu einer Stelle aus Martin Bubers Dissertation," *Kleinere Schriften* (Berlin: Schocken, 1937), pp. 240–44. This is a position which will appear as late as 1913 (see *Daniel: Dialogues on Realization,* trans. Maurice Friedman [New York: McGraw-Hill, 1965], p. 56); but by 1919 it will have been repudiated.
16. WM, BMM, pp. 184–85.
17. "Replies," PMB, p. 689.
18. "Dialogue," BMM, p. 13.

man—the unity of the I and Thou—is God." [19] But Feuerbach's I-Thou involves a Thou standing over against an I. Buber here considers the "over-against" to be merely preparatory: unity beyond distinction is consummation.[20] I-Thou thus appears early in Buber's thought, but it is the reverse of I-Thou as it will appear in the 1923 book by that title. He has to pass through a struggle with mysticism to reach that latter stage.

Mysticism, speculative and lived, provided Buber with roots in the life process. But his interest in mysticism was paralleled by his attempt to recapture his historical roots in the Jewish community. In 1897 he joined the ranks of the Zionist movement, which had recently gained international proportions under the capable leadership of Theodor Herzl. In keeping with the general nationalistic tendencies of the age, Zionism was concerned with establishing some sort of political identity for the Jewish community. Buber found in Zionism his "renewed taking root in the community." [21] He became a dedicated Zionist. To promote the artistic, poetic, and dramatic aspects of the movement, he founded a Zionist group at Leipzig in 1898.[22] In 1901 he joined the staff of the periodical *Die Welt,* which was the organ of the movement.[23]

But Zionism tended to go the way of most nationalistic movements, "making an idol of the people," [24] putting the needs of the group in place of dedication to universal truth and justice.[25] This is one reaction to the skepticism and relativism of the age, to the failure of speculative intelligence; the alternative reaction is an immersion in the universal through mysticism, which was the path Buber initially took.[26] This tendency found expression in the spiritual renewal of Judaism within Zionism, which Buber promoted; it led to a formal break at the Fifth International Zionist Congress in 1902 with the purely political orientation of the group which centered about Herzl.[27] This break provided the

19. Feuerbach, *Grundsätze,* sec. 62, p. 83.
20. "Ueber Jakob Boehme," *Wiener Rundschau,* V, No. 12 (1901), 251–53.
21. "My Way to Hasidism," HMM, p. 57.
22. Kohn, *Martin Buber,* p. 24.
23. *Ibid.,* pp. 48–49.
24. "Nationalism," IW, p. 224.
25. Kohn, *Martin Buber,* pp. 48–49.
26. Maringer, *Martin Bubers Metaphysik,* p. 15.
27. Robert Weltsch, "Einleitung," JSJ, p. xvii.

occasion for Buber and his group to found the Jüdischer Verlag for the promotion of works on Jewish culture.[28]

His participation in the Zionist movement presented Buber with two problems that were to be constants in his thought: What is the essence of Judaism? What constitutes genuine community? The latter question found early expression in the multi-volume series *Die Gesellschaft,* which appeared from 1905 through 1912 under Buber's editorship. The region explored here was, in the term employed in Buber's introduction, *das Zwischenmenschlichen,* the region between man and man that was to become the center of all his thinking.[29]

The question about the essence of Judaism merged with his interest in the mystics, for in mulling over the writings of the mystics and the Jewish tradition he was led to rediscover in Hasidism the vital roots of the Jewish mystical movement which he had previously met only in degenerate form. Buber was to become one of the major interpreters of the Hasidic movement; indeed, some would go so far as to say that his philosophy is basically an interpretation of Hasidism as the essence of Judaism, freed from dogma and cult rules, modified through the assimilation of the Enlightenment, and developed into a supra-confessional position. Buber speaks from Judaism as a Jew, but he speaks to all. And the message he speaks is the message of Hasidism.[30]

Hasidism came to him in a way that effected what can only be described as a conversion. He writes of his experience on a day in his twenty-sixth year when he was reading the *Zevaat Ribesh* of Israel Baal-Shem (1700–1760), the founder of Hasidism:

> . . . overpowered in an instant, I experienced the Hasidic soul. The primally Jewish opened to me, flowering to newly conscious expression in the darkness of exile: man's being created in the image of God I grasped as deed, as becoming, as task. And this primally Jewish reality was a primal human reality.[31]

As a result of that experience, he withdrew from Zionism for five years, giving himself over almost completely to the study of

28. *Ibid.,* p. xix.
29. Kohn, *Martin Buber,* p. 89, n. 1.
30. Arno Anzenbacher, *Die Philosophie Martin Bubers* (Vienna: Schendl, 1965), pp. 12–22; Kohn, *Martin Buber,* p. 86.
31. "My Way to Hasidism," HMM, p. 59.

Hasidism. This generated a long series of major works on Hasidism that extended from 1906 (*Geschichte des Rabbi Nachman*) to 1958 (*Hasidism and the Way of Man*); and in fact Buber was engaged in writing articles on Hasidism almost to the end of his life.[32]

Over the course of the two centuries since the time of its founder, Hasidism had produced a lengthy and variegated literature, composed chiefly of anecdotes. Buber attempted to sort out that literature and to arrive at an interpretation of Hasidism that could speak to the modern world. In his early years his principles of selectivity were heavily weighted in favor of the solitary mysticism of his own life concern. Later the emphasis would shift, especially in his Introduction to *Der grosse Maggid und seiner Nachfolge*.[33]

In Buber's first major Hasidic work, on Rabbi Nachman, he took special cognizance of the dialectical process of taking root, withdrawal, and return that characterized the Hasidic mystic's relation to the community. Cultural rootedness in a people built the foundations for Hasidic mysticism; the culmination occurred in the unfolding of the soul in ecstasy (as explicitly distinguished from the emptying of the soul which appeared in the writings of other mystics); and the fruit followed as a kind of by-product, informing the present life of the community the way the soul informs the body.[34] Hasidism thus appeared in direct contrast to those forms of mysticism in which escape from life and community and the achievement of *nirvana* as a total negation of the world and the self are the ideals of human nature. Buber admits rather obliquely, in a seemingly autobiographical passage in *Daniel* (1913), that the life-denying option tempted him. He says that there is the way of "that sublime wisdom which commanded one to strip off the world of duality as the world of appearance, 'like a snake skin,' and to enter the world of unity." This temptation "the faithful one" rejected. And yet this way "confirmed in him the striving for unity, for what he beheld detached guaranteed him fulfillment: . . . what revealed itself to him in self-collectedness must prove itself true for him in the

32. "Zur Darstellung des Chassidismus," *Merkur*, XVII (February, 1963), reprinted in W III, pp. 975–88.
33. Written in 1919. See below, p. 20.
34. "Die jüdische Mystik," *Die Geschichte des Rabbi Nachman*, W III, pp. 15–16.

scattered totality of his life-experience." [35] But he had not yet (1906) arrived at the latter position.

In his second major Hasidic work, *Die Legende des Baal-shems* (written in 1907, published in 1908), the ecstatic is still "above nature and above time and above thought," seeing all the individual things of the world as one, before whom the All is nothing and the Soul is all, and whose truest life is not among men. Service for one's fellow men is merely the path to this superior level: *"hitlahavut* [ecstasy] streams out of *avoda* [service] as the finding of God from the seeking of God." The ecstatic goes through life wandering "over the earth, dwelling in the silent distances of God's exile, companion . . . of the universal and holy happening of existence." But even the ecstatic unfolding is now seen as something to be transcended, for, at the highest rung, "ecstasy completes itself in its own suspension," when the ecstatic becomes "detached from all being and no longer . . . inflamed." [36] And so it appears that the unfolding of the soul which Buber saw in 1906 as a special characteristic of Hasidic mysticism eventually does terminate in its emptying. The ecstatic attains to the Nothingness of the Absolute,[37] which is the "form of the in between," "the power before creation" out of which creation flows. Apart from all comparison with men, where he is a limited, individual man, resting in himself as in nothing, he is without limits, "and God pours His glory into him." Blotting out his individuality, he sees himself as "a spark from the original soul," the whole of which is in each. He learns to love the whole. Detached from immediate relation to things, existing in the depths *between* creatures, i.e., in God, he creates "the carriage of God's majesty in the world." [38]

Nothing of what he says here is essentially out of harmony with the conception of an impersonal Godhead which develops in the human soul as Buber expounded it in his dissertation. But later [39] he comments that at this time (i.e., in the period between 1905 and 1907) the question of a dialogue between God and man—and thus of the personal character of God and the

35. *Daniel*, p. 137.
36. "The Life of the Hasidim," HMM, pp. 77–84.
37. *Ibid.*, pp. 94, 107.
38. *Ibid.*, pp. 115–21.
39. "Zur Geschichte des dialogischen Prinzips" (originally appeared in 1954), W I, p. 297.

distinctness of the partners in dialogue—gathered strength in his mind. But it arose in a mind still heavily preoccupied with mysticism; and it arose as a *question*, not yet as a position.

Though there are many parallels in the works of this period to the final positions in *I and Thou*, the major difference is that the community of love is formed apart from encounter, where individuals are preserved in their distinctness. Here, in this early work, real community is found in isolation, where the mystic is reduced to the Nothingness and the impersonal Godhead pours in Its glory and establishes the soul in community with all things.

The mystical theme is carried on in Buber's introduction to *Ekstatische Confessionen* (1909), a collection of the writings of the mystics of all ages. Anticipating a basic position of *I and Thou*, he sees the situation of everyday life composed of a whirlpool of feelings which are termed *the subject* and a whirlpool of objects which are termed *the world:* a dual situation with no intrinsic unity on either side of the dichotomy.[40] In two situations the self breaks out of this set of whirlpools to experience unity. One is the encounter with the Other—whether as a beloved person or a pile of stones—where all the powers of the soul are united and one experiences the identity of the I and the world. But in this sort of experience the object remains, flowing beneath the unity of the powers; and because the object remains, it soon drags the self back into the world of multiplicity. But there is another experience where the self, free of every Other, experiences its own unity. It is drawn up in ecstasy and appears to be one with God Himself.[41] However, ecstasy is essentially a matter of projection, for the I supports the World-I.[42] It was this that the Indian mystics saw so clearly. Beyond community with the Other, the self stands beyond the communicability of speech, for speech presupposes another which is addressed.[43] But as ecstasy dies, the Word is born: the ecstatic climbs down from the world of unity and infinity into the world of multiplicity and boundaries in order to proclaim, always inadequately, the unity

40. See below, pp. 40–42.
41. "Ekstase und Bekenntnis," *Die Rede, die Lehre, das Lied* (Leipzig: Insel, 1917), pp. 11–26.
42. ". . . das Ich . . . das Weltich trägt," *ibid.,* p. 18; see also pp. 15, 25, 28.
43. *Ibid.,* pp. 19–26.

beyond all multiplicity in the hope that it may become the unity of all multiple beings.[44]

In 1909 also, Buber edited *Reden und Gleichnisse des Tschuang-Tse*, to which he added an epilogue, "Die Lehre von Tao" ("The Teaching of the Tao"). *Lehre* ("teaching") belongs to the Eastern spirit, standing beyond the tensions of the "is" and the "ought" of Western thought, beyond its science and law. It is the Word which proceeds out of that unity which precedes all multiplicity. In that region of unity, the identity of the self with the All is realized. It is a unity which takes place neither in the object nor in the subject, for it is not a theoretical unity: rather it is the unity of life. Hence it is not located in thinking but in primal activity, so different from that which men usually call action as to be considered nonaction. It takes place in the solitude of wordless depths where "there is yet no Thou other than the I," where the unity of the world itself is experienced as a mere reflection of the unity of the self. Free of all distinction, the united man is joined to the Infinite, drawing the whole world with him into primal existence.[45]

It was likewise in 1909 that Buber was asked to lecture to the Bar Kokhba Circle in Prague on the nature of Judaism. The Circle was composed of young Jews, including Max Brod, Franz Kafka, and Hans Kohn.[46] These young men were caught up in the youth movement of the times, which rejected the rigidities of rational organizational society (*Gesellschaft*) and longed for a *Volksgemeinschaft* rooted in Blood, Soil, and the Destiny of the people. Typical of that movement was a widespread interest in the primitive sources of the people.[47] Buber's studies in the origins of Hasidism and its relation to the underground mystical piety that rooted itself in primeval biblical times prepared him for the task of addressing the youth movement within Judaism. Between 1909 and 1918 he delivered seven lectures on Judaism in Prague, Vienna, and Berlin. Out of this set of lectures emerged the *Reden über das Judentum*, which was published in 1923.

44. *Ibid.*, pp. 31–32. The significance of dealing with these views here will become evident in Chapters 3–5, where the parallels and differences with the position in *I and Thou* will be treated.

45. "The Teaching of the Tao," PW, pp. 32–56.

46. Kohn, *Martin Buber*, pp. 90–91.

47. Kohn, *Living in a World Revolution* (New York: Cardinal Pocket Books, 1965), pp. 62, 65–68.

Buber began these lectures by describing a path he himself had followed: the process by which an individual comes to be himself, establishing his own unity and self-identity. Initially caught up in the impressions and influences of the physical environment, he gradually comes to recognize his persisting corporeality as a substantial unity. This environment grows for him into a cosmos through the mediation of the *Volk*, which supplies him with the ordered structures of language and customs. This is the common world, for which the individual merely supplies the feeling tonality (*Gefühlsbetonung*). He comes to the realization of his own soul when the self-evident is *seen* for the first time, namely, his own continuity with the *Volk*. He realizes that his soul is not *with* his people: it *is* his people. And yet he realizes his authentic continuity only to the extent that he penetrates to and realizes his unique contribution to the totality.[48]

Here we have the same problem of the one and the many that provided the source of his dissertation: the individual *is* only in virtue of its relation to a higher totality, and it is that relation which constitutes the uniqueness of the individual. But what that relation is remains imprecise at this stage.

As in the case of the individual, so also with a people; one must penetrate to the core of its being to realize the contribution each makes to the totality. In the case of Judaism the core experience is of the *polarity* within the human soul—the polarity between the forming and the formless or, rather, between the forming and chaos, whether it be absolute chaos or chaos cloaked under decaying form.[49] The keenness of the polar experience provokes the *striving for unity*,[50] which is the striving toward form.[51] This, in turn, involves three mutually dependent notions: the ideas of unity, deed, and futurity.[52] Thus a sense of temporality opens up. Contrary to the space-dominated form-concept of the Greeks, which locks one up in the enjoyment of the present, the Jew moves in time, and ideas become tools for

48. "Das Judentum und die Juden," *Reden über das Judentum*, JSJ, pp. 12–18.
49. "Das Gestaltende," JSJ, p. 240.
50. "Das Judentum und die Menschheit," *Reden*, JSJ, p. 21.
51. "Das Gestaltende," JSJ, p. 243.
52. "Die Erneuerung des Judentums," JSJ, p. 33.

action, not ends in themselves.[53] Such is the a priori structure of the human soul as especially revealed in Judaism. The content varies from epoch to epoch, but always the experience of polarity provokes the struggle for unity through action aimed at the future. In striving for the unity of himself, the Jew comes to strive for the unity of his people; out of the unity of his people, he strives for the unity of all peoples and for the unity between the kingdom of man and the kingdom of subhuman life. Out of all this mighty striving for unity arose the notion of God as the Unity of all unities.[54] The task of man is to translate this from a notion into a reality,[55] to work at the *redemption of God*.[56] God is a projection of human striving. The transcendence of God is not yet recognized. God does not stand over against man and thus enter into dialogue with man; God comes to be in the striving of man for unity.[57]

In the following years Buber's preoccupation with origins and with Oriental wisdom continued, as is evident from the two works he edited in 1911 and 1913: *Chinesische Geister- und Liebesgeschichten* and *Kalewala* (the Finnish national epic). Out of his immersion in these subjects emerged Buber's first fully independent philosophical work, the first in which he was not concerned with interpreting the works of another but with completely expounding his own views. This work was *Daniel: Dialogues on Realization,* which appeared in 1913. *Daniel,* however, represents one stage in a transition that will lead from his early mysticism to his mature dialogical philosophy; this transitional period began in 1912 and was not completed until 1919.[58]

In *Daniel,* polarity, the *Urform* of the Jewish soul, and its consequent striving for unity again form the center of reflection. Out of the "glowing ground of the soul" as the longing for unity the wisdom of all ages arises to struggle with the problem of polarity, which appears in different modes in different ages:

53. *Ibid.,* pp. 40–41.
54. "Das Judentum und die Menschheit," JSJ, pp. 21–23.
55. "Das Judentum und die Juden," JSJ, p. 10.
56. "Das Judentum und die Menschheit," JSJ, p. 23; "Die Erneuerung des Judentums," JSJ, p. 40.
57. "Vorrede," *Reden,* JSJ, pp. 4–9.
58. "Replies," PMB, p. 689.

spirit and matter, form and matter, being and becoming, reason and will, positivity and negativity.[59] Long meditation on the age-old wisdom brought Buber through a number of stages during which he constantly wrestled with the problem of unity and multiplicity. The concluding pages of *Daniel* trace the stages through which "the faithful one" had to pass before he reached the "existentialist stage" represented in *Daniel*.[60]

The first stage was the way of the Hindu Vedanta, which consists in stripping off all dual tensions as mere appearance, involuting the soul in self-collectedness until it sees itself as *the* Unity. This had given Buber a sense of unity and the intense desire for it, but he now (1913) realized that this self-collectedness must preserve itself in the scattered totality of life, in apparent opposition to the isolated moment of ecstasy. Second was the way of German Idealism, which attained to the unity of the tensions of experience by thinking of them as sides to an underlying identity. This unity, however, was thought and not lived; something further is required. Third was the way of neutralizing all opposites through the teaching of the Tao, which undertakes the realization of unity in life. However, what has to be sought is a unity which preserves the opposites in their proper opposition: they are still joined together, and the tension itself constitutes their unification.[61]

The final level (final as of 1913) came one day when Buber was observing a piece of mica which had caught his attention. While he contemplated it, he experienced neither object nor subject but only unity. Looking at it again, he lost the unity but longed to recreate it. Closing his eyes, he bound himself with the object, and then his "I" first emerged. The first unity was indifferentiation; the second and presumably superior unity was unification created out of the realization of difference.[62]

Something more than ecstasy is required in this new stage: one needs *direction*. "He who surrenders himself to ecstasy with-

59. *Daniel,* p. 136.
60. Friedman, *Life,* pp. 27, 39.
61. *Daniel,* pp. 137–40. The identification of these stages as Hinduism, German Idealism, and Taoism follows Erich Przywara, "Judentum und Christentum," *Stimmen der Zeit,* CX (1925–26), 81–99.
62. *Daniel,* pp. 140–41. "Indifferentiation" translates *Ungeschiedenheit* and "unification" translates *Vereinigung* (W I, p. 74).

out direction is torn apart." He needs to find *his* way, the way of his individuality, through the multiplicity and duality of things, to gather up the flow of events into a totalized life. And yet that unification must not be conceived as a rational ordering in time by way of before and after, or in space by way of high and low, left or right, or in terms of causal connection. That is the *orienting* way, which can handle only the surface of things. When it seeks to become all-encompassing, it becomes thoroughly Godless. Rational patterning initially proceeds out of the deeper level of *realization*, where the commonplace is suddenly illuminated. In this way, Buber discovered, one gives birth, and out of this giving-birth and this discovery flow the structuring and utilization which belong to the realm of orientation.

In the primitive and the child, realization occurs, pure, uncluttered by aims—apparently in a unity which is indifferentiation. Maturity arises through orientation, which makes creativity possible. But the forms that spring out of this creation must always take their vitality from realization. In this way the genuine "I" arises, conscious of its difference, yet united to the whole in a higher way. In this way God Himself is realized.

So long as one develops in this way, one needs no external Thou. Even in experience of the Other, the Other seems to form the occasion for return to the self: the experience of the mica is completed when one closes one's eyes to the thing and realizes unity with it in oneself. The same type of experience with a tree draws one back to oneself, the tree being "transplanted out of the earth of space into the earth of the soul." *In* the self, with or without the Other, *the* unity is realized: God comes to birth, but now in the totality of life and not in the isolated moment of ecstasy apart from things.[63]

Much of this (with the notable exception of the becoming of God) was close to the formulation of *I and Thou*. But it was still in the realm of subjectivity, within the individual and not *between* being and being.[64]

In 1914 a collection of essays appeared, entitled *Ereignisse und Bewegungen* (*Events and Movements*), the most significant of which for our purposes is "Mit einem Monisten" ("With a Monist"). Here we have a clear transition from *Daniel* to *I and*

63. Cf. *Daniel*, pp. 53, 56, 64, 70, 71, 82, 91, 95, 98, 111, 140–41.
64. "Zur Geschichte des dialogischen Prinzips," W I, p. 299.

Thou. The realizing and orienting functions are now seen to have a complement in the structure of things: an active and a passive nature. The active nature corresponds to the realizing function of man; it is not manipulable, assimilable; it is "the confronting, the shaping, the bestowing in things." The passive corresponds to the orienting function; it is the usable, comprehensible, orderable—something one can take into oneself. If the active is not so assimilable, then it can be experienced, not in the self, but only in the encounter *between* the self and the Other. And such encounter brings out of the thing itself something that was not previously there. Thus one who truly meets the active in a thing knows in that thing the world and creates reality itself. "Reality is no fixed condition, but a quantity which can be heightened. Its magnitude is functionally dependent upon the intensity of our experiencing." But again, realization comes to maturity only when the rational power is fully developed.[65] It is thus no mysticism in the strict sense of the term but a philosophy of life which assimilates all its aspects, negating nothing, rationally ordering all that can be rationally ordered but open beyond all rationalism to the uniqueness of the individual, which is the bestowing shape, the self of things, beyond all rational structure.

Yet, "With a Monist" still exhibits a preoccupation with oneself and a care for those special moments of illumination. This preoccupation was decisively upset in 1914,[66] when, caught up in a moment of religious experience, Buber was interrupted by a friend whom he treated cordially but not with full concern. Subsequently he discovered that the man had really come to him for basic confirmation and that Buber had failed him through his relative indifference. Shortly afterward the man was killed in the war. Buber was never the same. As he described it:

> Since then I have given up the "religious" which is nothing but the exception, extraction, exaltation, ecstasy; or it has given me up. I possess nothing but the everyday out of which I am never taken. The mystery is no longer disclosed, it has escaped or it has made its dwelling here where everything happens as it happens. I know

65. "With a Monist," PW, pp. 25–28.
66. Dated by Buber's letter to Maurice Friedman, August 18, 1954, cited in Friedman, *Life*, p. 50, n. 3.

no fullness but each mortal hour's fullness of claim and responsi-bility.[67]

Claim and responsibility: these become the center of Buber's thought. "Being true to the being in which and before which I am placed is the one thing that is needful," Buber wrote in 1957. "I recognized this and what follows from it five years after setting down this small work ["The Teaching of the Tao" (1909)]. It took another five years for this recognition to ripen to expression." [68] 1914 was thus the key year.

In addition to this experience with the young man, Buber attained to a breakthrough in his relation to God. Hitherto God had been the impersonal Godhead coming to birth in the soul of the solitary mystic. But in the course of a discussion with a Reverend Hechler the question of faith in God arose, and then Buber saw that, "If to believe in God means to be able to speak of Him in the third person, I do not believe in God. If to believe in Him means to be able to speak to Him, I believe in God." [69] Along with his new self-exposure to the claim of the finite Other as it addressed him out of the context of the everyday, the independ-ence and demand of God Himself came to clarity in Buber's life.

From this point onward he rejected vigorously the mystical phase, which he came to see as indeed rooted in a genuine ecstatic experience of the all-inclusive and all-absorbing unity of the self that occurs in detachment from the life of day-to-day experience. But because of this detachment one loses the sense of the *principium individuationis* which comes only through encounter with the Other and through location in the temporal stream from birth to death. In ecstasy "the great dialogue be-tween the I and Thou is silent." Since no boundaries are visible in the mystical experience, the ecstatic tends to confuse the core of the experience with an experience of the All. He sees his unity as *the* unity. Hence he views this special experience as "higher" and everything else as, at best, preparation for, at worst, hin-

67. "Dialogue," BMM, p. 14.
68. "Foreword," PW, p. xvi.
69. *Begegnung*, p. 35. Translation mine. The question of the possibility of dialogue with God had arisen early in his life and was especially stimulated from 1905 on by his work with Hasidism. See "Zur Geschichte des dialogischen Prinzips," W I, p. 297.

drance to, his mystical consummation.[70] "This is certainly an exalted form of being untrue, but it is still being untrue." Such an experience is "not above but beneath the creaturely situation." [71]

Thus, between 1912, when he was engaged in the writing of *Daniel,* and 1919, when he was working on *I and Thou,*[72] many experiences came together into a unitary experience, which, from then on, formed the center of his thought.[73]

From 1916 to 1922 he undertook a kind of "spiritual asceticism" that would not terminate until the definitive draft of *I and Thou* had been completed. The only other major work that gained his attention was further study on Hasidism, out of which emerged, in 1921, *Der grosse Maggid und seine Nachfolge.* In the Introduction to this work (written in 1919) a reappraisal of Hasidism appears, a shift in the principle of selectivity. It is no longer solitary mysticism that is seen as the goal. "The ascetic ecstasy is . . . not of a divine but of a demonic nature. One shall not murder the 'evil urge,' the passion in itself, but serve God *with it.*" The "asceticism which strains after the void" indeed found its way into Hasidism, but it was mastered by "the inwardness . . . of turning and transformation of the world, . . . hallowing the everyday. . . . No longer a set action but the dedication of all action became decisive."

The core principle here is not the coming-to-be of the impersonal Godhead in the depths of the soul; rather it is "the double-directional relation of the human I and the divine Thou, . . . the reality of reciprocity, . . . the *meeting.*" But "one cannot come to God except through nature." Not in solitary subjectivity but in the subjective-objective event of meeting, in response to the creaturely Other, the unification (*Yihud*) of the world is achieved. And God Himself, the Unity without multiplicity, comes to dwell in this unification of multiplicity. With the recognition and response to the otherness of the Other, the otherness of God comes to be conceived. Previously Buber had thought in terms of subjectivity, for which the finite Other, at best, played

70. "Foreword," PW, pp. xv, xvi. See "Dialogue," BMM, pp. 24–25.

71. "Dialogue," BMM, p. 25.

72. The first sketch of this work had already been developed in 1916. See "Zur Geschichte des dialogischen Prinzips," W I, p. 298.

73. "Replies," PMB, p. 689; "Postscript," *I and Thou,* pp. 123–24.

an instrumental role and within which God Himself became real. Now he holds for the transcendence of God along with the intrinsic claim of the finite Other. God Himself is fateless, but He chooses to enter into the fate of the world: He awaits the action of man, which makes possible His coming to dwell in the world. Man is responsible for God's fate in the world. "World history is not God's game but God's fate." So there is the eternal form of divine unity, ever transcendent; and there is likewise the dynamic form of divine unity, the divine immanence. And this latter depends upon man's healing the world through meeting with his fellow creatures. The divine immanence is not accomplished by God alone, nor by man alone, but by man and God as they cooperate in creation. "The creature waits for him. God waits for him. From him, from 'below,' the impulse toward redemption must proceed. Grace is God's answer." [74]

Shortly after this Introduction to *Der grosse Maggid* was written, the rough draft of *I and Thou* was completed. In his own mind Buber had achieved the decisive clarity. It remained to work it out in final form. The new center represented a complete reversal of his earlier mystical tendencies. According to the mystic, the essential reveals itself in silence: God, world, and self are united without distinction. In the new position, God, world, and self stand facing one another, joined in their differences through the word they utter. The new philosophy is thus *Sprachphilosophie.*[75]

With this new center fixed, Buber's other works followed, clarifying his position in the face of objections and explaining it by means of examples, e.g., *Zwiesprache* in 1929, or criticizing views close to it from which he had drawn inspiration, e.g., *Die Frage an den Einzelnen* in 1936, where he considers Kierkegaard and Stirner, and *Das Problem des Menschens* in 1938, which deals with the history of philosophical anthropology and where Kierkegaard, Scheler, and Heidegger receive special attention. He likewise worked out the application of his core notions to education, as in *Rede über das Erzieherische* in 1926 and *Ueber Charaktererziehung* in 1939; to political and social thought, as in *Pfade in Utopia* in 1950 (Hebrew original, 1944), *Zwischen Gesellschaft und Staat* in 1950, and *Geltung und Grenze des*

74. "The Spirit and Body of the Hasidic Movement," OMH, pp. 117–34.
75. Kohn, *Martin Buber,* p. 240.

politischen Prinzips in 1953; to psychiatry in *Heilung aus der Begegnung* in 1952 and "Schuld und Schuldgefühle" in 1957; to ethics, as in *Bilder von Gut und Böse* in 1952. Toward the end of his life he became more preoccupied with the anthropological foundations; the major results of this interest appeared in scattered essays between 1950 and 1962 and were collected in 1963 under the heading *Beiträge zu einer philosophische Anthropologie.*

Work on the social consequences of his position dovetailed with his renewed participation in the Zionist movement and produced a wealth of essay collections: *Kampf um Israel* (1933, a collection of essays from the period 1921–32), *Die Stunde und die Erkenntnis* (1936, a collection from 1933–35), *Israel und Palästina* (1944), and *An der Wende* (1951, essays written between 1939 and 1951).

The final important strand in his work emerged shortly after the publication of *I and Thou*. Buber saw that man's answerability before the living God for his response to the situation found its keenest expression in the Hebrew Bible. In 1924 he joined with Franz Rosenzweig to begin a complete translation of the Old Testament according to a new set of principles for translation developed jointly in *Die Schrift und ihre Verdeutschung* (1935). The resultant work has been considered on a par with the Lutheran Bible and, along with the latter, as having no peer in the German language.[76]

At twenty-five, Buber discovered Hasidism; at forty-five, the Bible. And the Bible became for Buber's later life what Hasidism had been to his earlier life: his primary source of inspiration.[77] Out of this interest came a series of major biblical studies: *Königtum Gottes* (1932), *Der Glaube der Propheten* (Dutch original in 1940), *Moses* (Hebrew original in 1945), and *Sehertum* (1955)—all this alongside numerous shorter essays on biblical subjects. The encounter between Hebrew and Christian faith is examined in *Zwei Glaubensweisen* (1950), and the problem of God in the modern world appeared in 1953 in *Gottesfinsternis.*[78]

76. Eugen Biser, "Martin Buber," *Philosophy Today*, VII, No. 2 (1963), 108b.

77. Kohn, *Martin Buber*, pp. 255–56.

78. See the Bibliography at the end of this book for further details on English translations and other bibliographical data.

Since he was an authentic *Lebensphilosoph,* Buber's implication in life could not stop short with thinking and writing about it. His thinking about unity was in mutual relation to his attempt to achieve it in practice. We have seen him struggle with the problem in his own life, and, during the period following the composition of *Daniel,* events of great significance were unfolding around him. World War I broke out, the result of the retreat of spirit from life. Human life rallied about the banners of extreme nationalism, disdaining the universality of spirit. Catastrophe was inevitable.

Within Judaism the Zionist movement followed suit, continuing to develop along the lines of nationalism, in spite of Buber's great efforts to develop a universal sense within Zionism. The Balfour Declaration of 1917 added a new factor to the Zionist debate: Palestine was to be opened to the Jews. The people could once again join land, people, and culture into a real unity of life. The discussions which centered on this point received decisive stimulus through the periodical *Der Jude,* of which Buber was editor.

The International Zionist Congress of 1921 was the first such congress to meet after the Balfour Declaration. Here Buber was conspicuous by his strong opposition to extreme nationalism as "group egoism," the symptom of a serious disease among the people, "the indication of a fundamental lack in the life of the nation, a lack of unity, freedom, and territorial security." [79] Judaism cannot look upon itself as nationalistic in this sense even in view of its own self-conception as a "chosen people." The idea of election "does not indicate a feeling of superiority, but a sense of destiny," of a contribution which Israel is called upon to make to the nations at large.[80] And Buber thought that this contribution could be realized by a return to the land and by the establishment of a community of workers who would embody the authentic social uprightness announced by the Prophets. To that end he joined forces with the Hapoel Hazair group, out of which the later Kibbutzim were to spring.[81]

Even prior to the solution of the internal form of the new Palestinian Jewish community, there was the problem of its external relations with the Arab nations, who denied the Jewish

79. "Nationalism," IW, pp. 217–19.
80. *Ibid.,* p. 223.
81. Weltsch, "Einleitung," JSJ, p. xxx.

claim to the land which the Arabs had inhabited for centuries. Buber worked incessantly to solve that problem, even to the very end of his life, both as an individual and later as a member of the *Ichud* (the Hebrew term for unity, also transliterated as *Yihud*), an Arab-Jewish league for the establishment of a binational state.[82]

In preparation for the establishment of the new community, Buber saw education as the essential task. In 1923 he became professor of Jewish religion and ethics at the University of Frankfort and, with Paul Natorp, Franz Rosenzweig, and Eugen Rosenstock, formed the nucleus of the Patmos Circle, out of which emerged in 1926 the periodical *Die Kreatur*.[83] An intensely spiritual Jewish culture began to grow.

But when the National Socialists came to power in Germany in 1933, the education of the people at large reached a crisis. The Jews were turned out of the schools and were forced into their ghettos. The immediate problem was to set up a viable educational system, and in this task, again, Buber was at the center. He resigned from the University of Frankfort to devote himself completely to this work,[84] taking over the directorship of the *Lehrhaus* at Frankfort that had been founded by Franz Rosenzweig. A circle gradually formed about Buber, finding its center of meaning in biblical studies.[85]

In 1934 Buber delivered a lecture on "The Power of the Spirit" in which he contrasted paganism, Christianity, and Judaism. The occasion was the emergence of the new paganism, which glorified the objective elemental forces of blood and soil and the subjective elemental urges of hunger, sex, and the will-to-power. This neopaganism was the result of the severance of spirit from life in the modern world. In the role of detached intellect, spirit attempted to coerce the vital powers. In Pauline Christianity (as distinguished for Buber from the Christianity of Jesus) spirit and life are separated, with the spirit elevated in holy detachment and life negated. Judaism united spirit as human conscious totality in order to hallow the elemental urges

82. "Israel and the Command of the Spirit," IW, pp. 253–57.
83. Kohn, *Martin Buber*, p. 238.
84. Weltsch, "Einleitung," JSJ, pp. xxxv ff.
85. Weltsch, "Nachwort," in Hans Kohn, *Martin Buber*, pp. 423–24.

and forces in the service of God.[86] As such, Judaism has something essential to offer to the modern world, split between neopaganism and Christianity.

After such a lecture, for obvious reasons, the German authorities forbade Buber to lecture in public.[87] By 1938 they had clamped down on all his activities. With his work no longer possible, Buber emigrated to Palestine. This was unfortunate for Buber's influence upon the Jewish community. The generation of German Jews whom he had helped form was virtually annihilated by the Nazis. The Palestinian community was split between the secularists and the orthodox, who equally rejected him. His most decisive influence has been upon Christian thinkers.[88]

In Palestine Buber immediately assumed the chair of social philosophy at the Hebrew University of Jerusalem. Many persons had wished that he be given a lectureship in biblical studies, but that possibility had been ruled out by his negative attitude toward orthodoxy.[89] At the university he developed the lectures which were eventually to be published as *Das Problem des Menschens* and *Pfade in Utopia*. The latter grew out of his studies of the *Kvuza*, the Jewish village commune in Palestine.[90] He likewise went forward with his biblical studies.

Alongside his dedication to university education, the centrality of the education of the people at large never left him. After the war, in 1949, he founded the Institute for Adult Education, which trained teachers for an adult education that was not an extension of the academic life but had as its purpose the formation of a type of man fitted for the task of the historical situation. It emphasized a teaching method based on personal contact and living together in community. Instruction was to be carried on, not in general classes, but individually and in accordance with the needs of each person. It was a concrete instrument for developing the unity in multiplicity that had been Buber's con-

86. "The Power of the Spirit," IW, pp. 175–81.
87. "Preface," IW, p. 6.
88. Malcolm Diamond, *Martin Buber, Jewish Existentialist* (New York: Oxford, 1960), p. 169.
89. Weltsch, "Nachwort," p. 450.
90. "Foreword," *Paths in Utopia*, trans. R. F. C. Hull (Boston: Beacon Press, 1960), p. vii.

stant object of concern. Its purpose was to fashion from many individuals, with differing interests and even differing world views, a genuine community bound together by mutual concern and to furnish in this way a model community for all mankind. This indeed is the mission of Israel to the world as Buber saw and practiced it.[91]

At the end of the war he began a series of lecture tours. He visited Europe in 1947, America in 1951–52, Switzerland and Germany in 1953–54, England and Germany in 1956, and America once more in 1957–58. In 1951, at the age of seventy-three, he retired from the university and began to gather together his works in larger collections: *Hinweise* (1953); *Schriften über das dialogische Prinzip* (1954); *Hasidism and Modern Man* (1958); the completed Bible translation (1961); the three volumes of the *Werke*—Volume I, *Schriften zur Philosophie* (1962), Volume II, *Schriften zum Chassidismus* (1963), and Volume III, *Schriften zur Bibel* (1964); *Der Jude und seine Judentum* (1963); and *Nachlese* (1965). These collections, an impressively diversified corpus, represent, on the whole, the works Buber could still stand by today.[92]

The *Nachlese* collection, completed in February, 1965, gathered together the few significant essays not appearing in the other collections. In June of the same year Martin Buber died at the age of eighty-seven. His work was finished; he had drawn together his major works, whose essential concern was with drawing-together, with the unity of man with himself, with his fellow men, with nature, and with God. But the center of that work appeared in *I and Thou,* and to the analysis of that work we shall now turn.

91. Maurice Friedman, "The Existential Man: Buber," in Paul Nash *et al.* (eds.), *The Educated Man* (New York: John Wiley, 1965), p. 380.
92. "Nachwort," *Nachlese,* p. 261.

2 / The Form of *I and Thou*

BUBER HAS SOMETIMES been characterized as a philosopher, sometimes as a mystic, sometimes as a prose poet, and
sometimes as a theologian. Buber rejects the last label, since he
offers no doctrine on God but only a set of experiential observations on man's relation to God. He describes his own thinking as
atypical, but, if one has to label him, he prefers to be called a
philosopher since reason, elaborating on his fundamental experiences, figures so strongly in his work.[1] He has even gone so far as
to describe himself, in the time of transition between his "existentialist" and his "dialogical" periods, as a *rationalist* who insists on weaving the net of reason as tightly as possible. And yet
he likewise claims to be a rationalist who constantly breaks
through the carefully woven net in his poetic soaring toward the
Infinite. However, despite his early fascination with mysticism,
he categorically rejects the label "mystic," [2] of which he offers a
lengthy critique in the longest section of *I and Thou.*

I and Thou itself weaves together the various strains of
Buber's thought into a work which is at once philosophical and
poetic, expository and dialogical. The philosophical effort itself
necessarily makes an object of every lived immediacy.[3] And since
it is Buber's aim to make us see this very immediacy, from time
to time the network of careful observations and meticulous distinctions is suddenly broken through by poetic apostrophe as

1. "Replies," PMB, pp. 689–90.
2. "With a Monist," PW, pp. 25–28.
3. "Replies," PMB, p. 689.

Buber hymns the Thou (§ 52) [4] or bemoans the dominance of the It (§§ 6, 32). Abstract analysis and concrete presence are welded together, yet even this may take place within the sphere of the solitary, monological thinker. Buber wants to bring us to dialogue, which presupposes the presence of the Other standing over against us. Hence the text is punctuated here and there with the interruptions of an unidentified Other, breaking the logical sequence of ideas (§§ 21, 26, 41), initiating a new line of exposition (§§ 13, 35, 39, 41, 42, 57), or stimulating the continuation of a theme the writer was developing (§§ 37, 48, 50). The presence of the Other, corroborating and interfering, hovers over the text.

The work itself is like a Thou, displaying a kind of poetic magic which leaves in the reader a sense of what Buber intends but likewise leaves many things unclear. Buber insists that any attempt to systematize his thought is unfaithful to his aim,[5] and yet he is aware that every Thou is fated to become an It (§ 22). Like any Thou in our experience, his work, too, has elements of structure which are analyzable. The attempt at analysis, though indeed fraught with the very serious danger of destroying the immediacy of experience, likewise puts us in a position of being able eventually to experience the immediate more profoundly. There is a kind of dialectical circle operative here, as there is in all relation to things of value. We can live in the immediacy of a painting or a musical performance. The attempt at analysis may threaten that blissful immediacy, but there comes a time when, through persistence in analysis, along with attention to immediacy, immediacy itself is deepened. The musical score, as Buber observes, is not the same as the musical performance (§ 28); and yet we may add that an understanding of the score may eventually enhance the appreciation of the performance. Furthermore, there is something more at stake here than a kind of consumer relation to the Thou which Buber attempts to present by his work. There is likewise the problem of a productive relation, through which we are enabled to bring forth the kind of works that can become Thou; and to achieve that, one must have knowledge of the factors that enter into the creative process. Buber himself understood the techniques involved in his own

4. See n. 6, below, for the system of referring to the text of *I and Thou*.

5. "Replies," PMB, p. 693.

creative work. The problem, as Buber himself saw it, was not one of curtailing the world of It, because, if man is to do his work in the world, precision and consequently objectification are necessary; but what ultimately matters is to learn to plunge the work into the truth of relation (§ 32).

As far as the over-all pattern of the work is concerned, there are two forms of covert articulation in the text: first, the whole is divided into three parts without any headings; second, within each part, sections are separated by asterisks. I have attempted to discern the logical outline which unites these sections and have provided titles for the logical divisions. And to facilitate reference to the text of *I and Thou,* I have numbered the asterisked sections in sequence from 1 to 61. The reader may find it convenient to do the same with his own copy of *I and Thou.* This should facilitate the close reference to the original required by the analysis presented in the next three chapters.[6]

The totality of *I and Thou* is a kind of romantic symphony in three movements, each with a different internal structure and rhythm. The chart on pages 30–31 presents the over-all structure in a schematic way, indicating the nodes in the text where the key terms appear with special emphasis, along with variant and related terms.

Part One lays down the basic themes in short, pregnant, aphoristic sentences (§§ 1–8). These basic themes will be repeated, often word for word, punctuating the work at different points throughout all three movements. The movement progresses by orchestrating these themes in different contexts, moving in a logically discernible way from the statement of basic themes (§§ 1–8) to a somewhat less curt treatment of the regions of relation (§§ 9–12), through a discussion of the characteristics of the Thou-meeting (§§ 13–21) to a lengthier exposition of the emergence of It in the worlds of the primitive and the child (§§ 22–28), and ending by drawing the themes together to give

6. The numbering follows the sections of the German text in W I, pp. 79–160. There is only one deviation from the English translation of Ronald Smith (New York: Scribner's, 1958): page 4, § 4. Smith omits the division as found in the *Werke* text beginning with "When *Thou* is spoken. . . ." In the German text this line begins what we shall number as § 5. The top of page 5 in the Smith text which reads, "It is said that man experiences his world," will then begin § 6 in our numbering sequence. The Smith text will henceforth be referred to as simply "Smith," followed by the page number.

THE STRUCTURE OF I AND THOU

KEY NOTIONS

BASIC OUTLINE

I. THE BASIC NOTIONS

Section Numbers	Outline
1–8	A. Basic Notions (§§1-8)
9–12	B. Regions of Relation (§§9-12)
13–21	C. Characteristics of the Thou-Meeting (§§13-21)
22–28	D. Emergence of the It (§§22-28)
29–30	E. Gathering the Themes Together (§§29-30)

Key Notions columns: WORD · REGIONS OF RELATION · RELATION · THOU · GOD · WORLD · I · IT

Labels:
IT — Thing, Object, Space and Time, Causality
I — Experience, Use, Feeling, Primitives, Child
RELATION — Presence, Totality, Immediacy, Grace, Mutuality
REGIONS OF RELATION — Forms, Men, Nature, Ideas
WORD — Between, Spirit

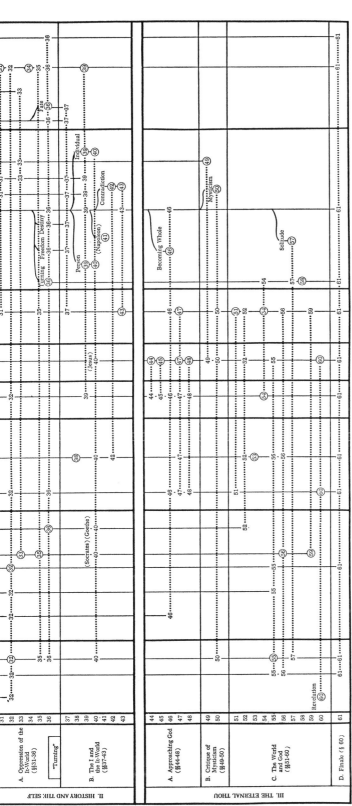

This chart correlates an index of key notions with the outline of *I and Thou*. The numbers listed under any given notion indicate the sections of Buber's text in which the notion occurs in a significant way. The circled numbers indicate the *major* focus of the section in question in each case. The uncircled numbers indicate merely that the notion in question appears in a significant role in the section so numbered but is not the center of focus. The dotted lines link together the notions treated in a given section, indicating that these are the basic concepts appearing in that section. The vertical lines under each term link the sections to the key terms, indicating that these are the sections in which the key terms appear. Terms related to the key notions appear under the key notions in question. For example: scanning horizontally, § 17 focuses upon *Presence and Immediacy* (notions connected with *Relation*); the section likewise treats of *It*, *Space and Time* (notions related to *It*), and *Use* (a notion related to *I*). Scanning vertically, *Immediacy* appears significantly in §§ 15, 16, 17, and 18 and is the major focus of these sections, while *Presence* appears in §§ 9, 12, 16, 17, 23, 29, 32, 36, 46, 47, 48, 51, 60, and 61, functioning as the center of attention in §§ 17 and 60.

a certain sense of completeness to the treatment. Here and there throughout this first movement hints of the pathos and struggle of the second movement appear in brief snatches where Buber speaks of escape from the onslaught of nothingness (§§ 18, 26, 29); and only a few traces of the central theme of the third movement—God, the eternal Thou—appear here likewise (§§ 9, 29). Though the movement ends resolved, it ends in a minor key with the pronouncement that the man "who lives with *It* alone is not a man." This will supply the theme for the second movement.

Part Two begins by accentuating the theme of the growth of the world of It. The sections become longer and heavier and the context more oppressive as the world of It is developed, up to the logical center of the movement (§ 36), where Fate appears. But in the same place, conversion, "turning," also appears, and attention shifts from the world of It to focus upon the man who is caught up in that world. The movement ends unresolved in a minor key with self-contradiction and the inward shudder it provokes. The central theme of the third part appears only once (§ 40), where the light of the authentic person shines through in Goethe and Socrates and, above all, in Jesus related to His Father.

Part Three again has an entirely different character, opening in an uplifting way with the Thou presented as opening to the eternal Thou. Attention then moves from theme to theme in developing the approach to God. By far the lengthiest treatment of the whole book appears in § 50, where Buber confronts the strongest opponent to his dialogical philosophy: the monological state of ecstasy where either the I or the Thou disappears in supposed unity. Once he passes through that encounter, the rest of the movement unfolds to its climax in § 61, where all the themes are gathered together and the philosophical symphony ends on the glorious note of redemption.

Our next three chapters consist of section-by-section analysis of the text of *I and Thou* in the light of the total corpus of Buber's works, though the works which preceded *I and Thou*, which were discussed in Chapter 1, receive less emphasis. The analysis leans more heavily upon the works which followed *I and Thou* as explicit attempts at clarification and development of its themes, and it is selective, being based upon a search for the ontological foundation. Hence it does not necessarily move line by line. When the text appears clear enough or deals with a subject tangential to the major concern, a more summary view is given. The focus is upon the ontological nodes of the text.

3 / Part One: The Basic Notions

SKETCH OF THE BASIC NOTIONS (§§ 1–8)

World (§ 1)

PART ONE BEGINS: "Die Welt ist dem Menschen zwie-fältig" ("To man the world is twofold"). Of the basic notions, "world" is the first to appear in the work, and it crops up again and again with varying but related meanings. Here in § 1 Buber uses it in the sense of the real totality of beings.[1] World in this sense will eventually be seen as set off from that which is not world, from some sort of transcendence.[2] World as real totality will thus be an immanent totality. Such a world, however, is not considered here in itself, but rather in its appearance to man.[3] Thus "the starting point of *I and Thou* is neither metaphysics nor theology but philosophical anthropology, the problem of man."[4] Indeed, for Buber, philosophical anthropology is the very center of his philosophy.[5] Hence in this, his central work, he considers the totality in its relation to man—as it appears to the human being.

World can appear as one of two human worlds, depending

1. Michael Theunissen, "Bubers negative Ontologie des Zwischen," *Philosophisches Jahrbuch,* LXXI, No. 2 (1964), 323.
2. "Von der Verseelung der Welt," *Nachlese,* p. 151.
3. IMB, p. 85.
4. Maurice Friedman, "Translator's Introduction," KM, p. 13.
5. "Replies," PMB, p. 693; WM, BMM, pp. 118–126.

[34]

upon the attitude of man. These are what he calls the "It" world (§ 6) and the world of "relation" (§ 8). The It-world, in turn, will have worlds constituted within it, depending upon the various regions of human relatedness: the cosmic world of consistency, the "erotic" world of interhuman sensitivity, and the world of value (§ 55)—all constructs of a sort, built upon the world of the senses. The world of the senses, in its turn, is unintelligible without reference to the world of objects perceived and the world of the percipient subject, as well as the world of their meeting, which is the world of sense phenomena.[6]

Yet even the world of sense phenomena does not appear as a *world* to the senses, for the senses yield only the immediate environment.[7] Even this sense world involves a type of human synthesis which combines the known with the unknown,[8] for the totality as such is not experienced. Neither the known nor the unknown involves simply one's own synthesis, but both are constituted in addition by the inclusion of the data and interpretations of the race.[9] When we refer to the data and interpretation of the race, we move into the question of cultural worlds: the world of the Greeks, the world of the Egyptians (§ 31). Such a cultural world is the mode of dwelling for a people in the world totality. It is this sort of world for which Buber generally reserves the term *cosmos*.[10]

The roots are clearly Kantian. Buber admitted toward the end of his life that he had always remained under the influence of Kant.[11] For Buber, as for Kant, the world of experience is a world of phenomena. Buber sees the world of the senses as a set of appearances that had passed through the filter of biological purpose (see below, pp. 46–48), and he sees the organized world of thought as relative to man's adjustment: neither gives us the thing-in-itself.[12] But, with Kant, Buber admits the thing-in-itself, the x of whose existence we are aware. And yet, going

6. EG, p. 5.
7. "Distance and Relation," KM, pp. 60–61.
8. *Ibid.*, p. 62.
9. WM, BMM, p. 155; Letter to Friedman, February 19, 1963, cited in Friedman, "Translator's Introduction," KM, p. 24; EG, p. 42.
10. "What Is Common to All," KM, p. 105; §§ 36, 55, 61.
11. IMB, p. 21.
12. "Bergson's Concept of Intuition," PW, p. 83; "Distance and Relation," KM, pp. 60 ff.

beyond Kant, Buber adds that we likewise know that the thing-in-itself *meets* us; [13] and this meeting becomes of central importance in Buber's thought. It is in this meeting that Buber will locate the unconditioned character of philosophy, while the worlds of interpretation are all seen as conditioned. [14] It is in terms of the intensity of meeting that the actuality of the world in its appearance to man deepens. [15]

We see here a tension between encounter with the individual and reference to the totalities within which the individual comes to be located. The implications of this relation will be explored as the analysis develops. At this point, in the beginning of the text, the focus is upon the twofold way in which the *totality* appears to man. After a brief reference to the world again in §§ 7, 8, and 9, attention moves on to consider relation to an *individual*. Not until §§ 27–30 will attention again be given to the world, where the text moves back and forth from world to individual. Part Two will discuss the growth of the *world* of It and the struggle of the individual man with that world, while it is chiefly in § 54 of Part Three (with a brief reference in §§ 9 and 29 of Part One) that the *world* of Thou, of relation, is given central consideration.

Word (§§ 1–3)

Man's basic relationship to the world is an expression of his own self. Whether or not it issues forth in linguistic expression, such a relationship is the basic "word" (*Grundwort*) which man utters to whatever he meets. Since such a basic word involves a reference to the Other to whom it is "spoken," it is not an isolated expression but a relational term, a "combined word."

Such primary words, however, must not be considered as self-expressions in the sense of psychological projections. "When a primary word is spoken, the speaker enters the Word and takes his stand in it" (§ 3). "Word" is later (§ 32) revealed as spirit, which is not something "in" man but rather occupies the region between man and things (§ 50), [16] opening out as a relation to

---

13. "Man and His Image Work," KM, p. 157.
14. "Zur Situation der Philosophie," *Nachlese,* p. 138.
15. "With a Monist," PW, p. 28.
16. Smith, p. 93.

that which transcends the world.[17] Spirit is something which comes to man (§ 32) and which man is to obey (§ 35). It is that out of which language (*Sprache*) arises (§ 9). "Entering the word" for Buber is moving into those regions where spirit becomes manifest, either *in* man (§ 7) or *between* man and something other (§ 5). Spirit's manifestation *in* man occurs as a distillation out of its primary and original manifestation in the region between beings.

Such manifestations stem from the two "basic movements" of man: *Rückbiegung*, or bending back to oneself, and *Hinwendung*, or turning toward the Other.[18] The "backward-bending" movement develops into the attitude which considers the Other as an object existent for the self; the movement of "turning-toward" develops into an attitude in which the Other is allowed to put its claim upon the self. In *Daniel*, Buber termed these the orienting and the realizing functions, respectively.[19] When we persist in the movement of "backward-bending" and develop our pragmatic orientation within which the Other fits, we form an attitude where the Other is in itself value-neutral and is an object for my projects. The value-neutral Other is (is treated as) the *neuter* Other; hence, one basic word is I-*It*. When we persist in the movement of "turning-toward" and develop the realizing function where the Other becomes the revered-in-itself, we form an attitude which lays the basis for what Buber terms, accordingly, I-*Thou*.

In the I-It relation, Buber remarks, "für Es auch eins der Worte Er und Sie eintreten kann" ("For It one of the terms He or She can also be substituted"). *Sie* in German can carry four meanings: "she," "they," and "you" (singular and plural). In view of the general grounding of grammatical relations Buber is here expressing, one wonders if the *Sie* might not carry all four meanings here: any "you" (singular or plural) that does not really mean "Thou" is really "It"; every "she" or "they" is really "It." "We" is not given explicit treatment here, but it would follow the general twofold structure of the I, depending upon the attitude of the group. Hence there would be either a collectivity of internally alienated individuals thrown together or a genuine

17. "Von der Verseelung der Welt," *Nachlese*, p. 151.
18. "Dialogue," BMM, pp. 21 ff.
19. *Daniel*, p. 64.

community formed by living relation to a common center (§ 33).[20] We have here, then, a bit of "linguistic analysis" which attempts to push deeper than the Anglo-Saxon version often considers it necessary or even possible to go. Buber attempts to ground grammatical structure in fundamental human structure as it is related to the world.

Word is thus the sphere of the *Between,* of the primary relatedness binding man to the Other. It is the region of Spirit grounding man and yet capable of being articulated according to the way man takes his stand in it. Out of this stand grammatical expressions arise.

Formation of the I (§§ 1–3)

From his pithy consideration of the primary words, I-Thou and I-It, Buber turns to the first of the partners in these relations: the I. Since man's two basic relationships to the world are fundamentally different modes of self-expression, two radically different meanings of the I are found. Some commentators [21] object that there is no evidence for two I's. But so much depends upon what we mean by "I" and upon how radically we take the meaning of the difference between the two I's. Buber would not deny that the two I's he speaks of here appear in the same *man* (cf., e.g., § 39). If that be the case, then the difference between the two cannot be taken with absolute radicality, for they are distinguished within the same entity. But far from settling the issue, this "solution"—like most philosophical solutions—only opens up new questions. What then is meant by the "sameness" of this same entity? Here we come to grips with the problem of the analogicity of identity. Even if we grant that every entity is identified with itself, the evidence seems to suggest that some entities (e.g., men) are *more* self-identified than others (e.g., stones) and that, within the same entity, at certain times a person may be more self-identified than at other times, so that we find ourselves occasionally forced to tell those who are of concern to us to "get hold of themselves." Buber tries to specify the situation within which maximum self-identification is achievable. He affirms at this point that it is in relation to the Thou that this occurs. I-Thou involves the whole of one's being;

20. Smith, p. 45.
21. Anzenbacher, *Die Philosophie Martin Bubers,* p. 101.

I-It can never involve the whole. Though the grounds for this are not fully explicit, a basis may be suggested that is in keeping with the evidence Buber provides.

All awareness is manifestation of otherness. Simultaneous with that manifestation there emerges the sense of selfhood in terms of which otherness is specifiable. There is no specifiable I without the Other in virtue of which the I is specifiable; but likewise there is no *manifest* Other without the I in virtue of which the Other is manifest. The self and the Other are dialectically related.

Now the I-It relation is revelation of the Other, not wholly in itself, but as object for one's use (speculative or pragmatic conquest). The Other is here manifest as a function of the self— biologically in terms of the sense functions, and perspectively-intellectually in terms of interpretation, which for Buber is always conditional. Hence, although otherness is manifest, it is not the Other as *other* but as *Other-for-me*. But if otherness is not wholly manifest, neither is selfhood. The Other is referred back to the given structure of man that determines the character of the manifestation.[22]

Man, however, is a creature of distance from his own givenness,[23] of orientation toward the Infinite,[24] of fundamental transcendence. In virtue of that distance, the revelation of otherness is capable of development, and hence selfhood is capable of increase. The term of that revelation is the manifestation of the Other wholly as other, apart from speculative or pragmatic conquest. Revelation of the Other-in-totality presupposes and grounds, in a simultaneous mutual act, selfhood-in-totality (cf. §§ 13, 14). Thus: "The primary word I-Thou can only be spoken with the whole being. The primary word I-It can never be spoken with the whole being" (§ 2). Obviously, what "the whole of one's being" means remains to be determined, except abstractly in terms of the dialectic of relation. What is the total otherness of the Other? What is the full selfhood of the self?

It is essential to call the reader's attention once more to the

22. Contrary to Leslie Paul (*The Meaning of Human Existence* [New York: Lippincott, 1950], p. 148), the problem with the I-It relation is not that it is *other* but that it is not *wholly* other, considered in terms of man's conscious relation to it.
23. "Distance and Relation," KM, pp. 60 ff.
24. "With a Monist," PW, p. 27; WM, BMM, p. 121.

fact that Buber does not imply that there are no entities prior to, and grounding, the revelation of otherness. He is only claiming that there is no (*self-conscious*) I and no *manifest* Other without relation. There is, however, man and some other entity "underlying" the manifestation, but that will be considered later (§ 27).

The Structure of the Other (§§ 4–8)

Taking up an attitude as the fundamental mode of self-expression is the basic activity of man. For Buber such attitudes are not static states but fundamental activities ("verbs") (§ 4). Not all such activities are goal-directed (*zielende*), not all are constituted by the subject-object relation. Perceiving, feeling, imagining, thinking, and willing are all partial activities of man, distinct from one another and characterized by the structure of the subject-object relation: each particular act intends some object which is an aspect of the Other structured in terms of the act. And all such activities for Buber are seen as taking place *in* man as the mirroring-back of man's own biological and intellectual needs through the Other. Each object is located within a humanly constructed frame of reference relative to other objects (§ 5) and is broken up into its various perceptible or interpretable aspects (§ 10). Inner and outer, open and secret items of such pulverized experience can then pile up within that framework. The world stands there as *Gegen-stand*, allowing itself to be manipulated (§ 7).

This is what founds the world of It. Buber terms it "experience" (*Erfahrung*) and then plays on the etymological root of the term in *fahren*, "to travel." To travel is precisely to experience only the surface of life, since real intimacy is possible only through a mode of prolonged dwelling with the Other (§ 6). Buber uses another term for experience to describe the I-Thou relation: *Erlebnis*, from *leben*, "to live" (§ 23),[25] signifying authentic human living (§§ 11, 14).

When "Thou" is spoken, one meets the incomparable. There is no reflective categorizing, dividing, and separating, in terms of which one can orient oneself; there is no planning.[26] Buber

25. Smith, p. 21; *Daniel*, p. 66.
26. Carl Frankenstein argues that "Thou" concerns the Other as addressed by the self and thus not wholly as other. It is only when

negates all the intentional structures of experience in their multiplicity and correspondingly points to a negation of their objective correlates in the intentionally manifest aspects of the Other. In the I-Thou relation the undivided self meets the undivided Other. The multiplicity of intentional acts and objective aspects are present only implicitly, in solution, occupying the fringe rather than the focus of consciousness.[27] One turns to the Other and stands in a relation of undivided to undivided which constitutes the actualized realm of the Between (§§ 5, 7).

The Between actualized in relation is the central notion of Buber's thought. Hence this position has been described as a "negative ontology of the Between." [28] The notion of the Between carries two significant elements. First, it points to the self-transcendent character of the act whereby one relates to the Thou. Second, it points to the ultimate inaccessibility, i.e., the real *otherness* of the Thou.[29]

Buber wants to remove all psychologizing tendencies which would interpret away the essential character of the act; relation, he insists, is not psychological so much as it is ontological, i.e., a relation to the being of the Other.[30] But he likewise wants to preclude the kind of mystical absorption in which the self and the Other seem to melt together (cf. Chapter 1, above). For Buber the Between is a realm which is neither objective nor subjective nor the sum of the two.[31] If one were to remove all

the Other is seen as not-I that it addresses me as existent in itself ("Du und Nicht-Ich: Zu Martin Bubers Theorie des Dialogs," *Stimmen der Zeit*, CLXXVIII, No. 11 [1966], 356 ff.). This reverses Buber's perspective, however, since it takes its point of departure from the self and thus mediates the immediacy of relation, reflectively hampering the spontaneity of reaching out toward the Other. Furthermore, to say "Thou" is precisely to lay oneself open to the claim of the Other.

27. See Theunissen, "Bubers negative Ontologie," p. 321.

28. *Ibid.*

29. Hence the complete inaccuracy of Jacob Agus' claim that the I-Thou relation is "just short of unity" (*Modern Philosophies of Judaism* [New York: Behrmans, 1941], p. 254). It is *precisely* the rejection of such unity that Buber is maintaining—all the more so because he had earlier held just such a position. Leslie Paul (p. 139) falls into the same error when he interprets the basis of relation as desire "for the merging, not simply for the meeting of two beings."

30. Buber in Robert C. Smith, "Correspondence," p. 248.

31. "Replies," PMB, p. 707.

that belongs to the object and all that belongs to the subject, there still would remain the Between.[32] For Buber there is another dimension,[33] which is man's opening toward God (cf. §§ 9, 44). Meeting with the individual Thou is that which *grounds*[34] the world of relation. But meeting with God is that which binds the moments of Thou-relation into the *world* of Thou (§ 54).

REGIONS OF RELATION (§§ 9–12)

General Considerations (§ 9)

THE WORLD OF RELATION has its root in three spheres of human relatedness: our life with nature (as the region of the subhuman), with other men, and with *geistige Wesenheiten.* The first two regions are readily identifiable in terms of specific entities which enter into our field of perception. The third is more difficult to discern. And the difficulty is not eased by Smith's translation of the phrase as "spiritual beings."

In the sections which immediately follow, Buber discusses, in turn, our relation to nature in the case of encounter with a tree (§ 10), our life with men (§ 11), and encounter with a form (*Gestalt*) which is the source of art (§ 12). ("Form" here is transempirical but demands embodiment in a specific material.) The same three relations are treated in §§ 19 and 22. In these three sections (§§ 10–12) "art forms" seems initially to be what Buber means by *geistige Wesenheiten.* But in his explicit treatment of *Geist* ("spirit") in § 32, Buber deals with *three* areas in which the activities of spirit are realized: not only in art, but also in knowledge and in "pure effective action, without arbitrary self-will." [35] This triad throws light upon the three modes of

32. "The Word That Is Spoken," KM, p. 112.
33. WM, BMM, p. 204. See Karl Heim, *Christian Faith and Natural Science*, trans. N. H. Smith (New York: Harper Torchbooks, 1953), for a consistent development of the notion of a new dimension for Thou-relations.
34. Smith's translation of *stiftet* here as "establishes" is misleading, since the development of the Thou-relation into a *world* of relation requires something more.
35. ". . . das reine Wirken, die Handlung ohne Willkür." Most commentators give the problem of this third region of encounter insufficient attention. Anzenbacher (*Die Philosophie*, p. 92) calls this simply the region of *Kunstphilosophie;* Friedman (*Life*, p. 74) sim-

response to the *geistige Wesenheiten,* which appear compactly and cryptically in § 9 as "forming, thinking, acting." [36] These three modes of response seem to correspond to three of the basic potencies of the soul mentioned elsewhere: art, knowledge, and love.[37] And in § 55, speaking of the regions of relation again, Buber mentions "the mute proclamation of the creature" (relation with nature), "man's loving speech" (relation with fellow men), and "form's silent asking" (relation with the *geistige Wesenheiten*). Art, knowledge, and "pure effective action" are thus the regions of the *forms of the spirit.* Hence the translation "forms of the spirit" is here proposed for *geistige Wesenheiten* in place of Smith's confusing "spiritual beings." [38]

Taking our stand in one of the two *Grundworte* is stepping into the region of spirit. In our response to what emerges from this stance, we move from the fundamental word (*Wort*), which is prelinguistic, to articulate speech (*Sprache*). Hence for Buber the source of speech lies in our response to encounter with the forms of the spirit, though the encounter itself is supralinguistic. On the other hand, in our relation with nature the encounter is

ply mentions it without explanation in summarizing Part Three of *I and Thou;* he passes it by without mention in his summary of Part One (*ibid.,* pp. 57–61) and fails to tie it up with his brief summary of knowledge, art, and action in Part Two (*ibid.,* p. 63).

36. "Bildend, denkend, handelnd." "Shaping" is preferable to "forming" as a more adequate translation of *bildend,* since for Buber "form" takes on a kind of technical meaning which covers all three modes and not merely art.

37. "Man and His Image Work," KM, p. 168.

38. Friedman (*Life,* p. 74) offers "intelligible essences"; but "intelligible" carries with it connotations of intellect, and Buber has something wider in mind than that; likewise, the term "essence" has the same type of connotation as correlate to intellect. Paul Pfuetze offers "intelligible forms" (*Self, Society, Existence* [New York: Harper Torchbooks, 1954], p. 157). "Form" suggests something broader than essence, for form includes all aspects of human creativity; but "intelligible" is unacceptable for the reasons given. "Spirit" and "spiritual" (*Geist* and *geistig*) in German thought furnish an exact correlate to "form." Hence the solidity of the suggested translation "forms of the spirit," in terms not only of Buber's text, but of German philosophical usage in general. [After this text was completed, Ronald Smith's book, *Martin Buber,* appeared in the Makers of Contemporary Theology Series (Richmond, Va.: John Knox Press, 1967). Smith mentions (p. 16, n. 19) that Buber told him, in a letter of December 6, 1957, that *geistige Wesenheiten* means "spirit in phenomenal forms." Q.E.D.]

sublinguistic.[39] It is only in our relation with our fellow men that the relation itself is in the form of speech, i.e., in the give-and-take of the communication of meaning.

CHART 2

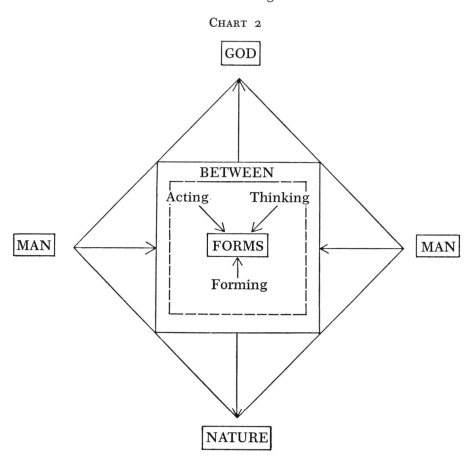

The primary line is the horizontal, indicating the meeting between man and man, rooted upward in God and downward in nature. The square in the center represents the Between, the open sphere of these relations articulated into a *cosmos* of forms of the spirit through reflective thinking, meaningful action, and the formation of works of art.

In treating of the three regions elsewhere,[40] Buber speaks of relation to nature, to man, and to the "transcending mystery of

39. "Postscript," *I and Thou*, pp. 124–26.
40. WM, BMM, p. 177.

Being" which the philosophers call the Absolute and believers call God. Here in § 9 he speaks of the eternal Thou as shining through all other relations. If we recall that spirit is relation to that which transcends the world, then we can understand relation to the forms of spirit as incipient relation to God. These forms appear through our relation to the human and subhuman entities we meet, drawing our relation beyond—or actually *within*—the immediate encounter to encounter with something beyond, something transcendent which speaks to us in and through all things. Such encounters break forth in the communicative embodiments through which we speak to one another (cf. § 56), drawing upon the potentialities of the soul for knowledge, art, and love and culminating in the evocation of the fundamental potency: faith in the transcendent Thou.[41]

This is a distillation out of Buber's own experience, which developed from many experiences of being (*Seinserfahrungen*) into one great experience of faith (*Glaubenserfahrung*).[42] From this he gained his insight into the way in which community is formed and the way in which it affects the individual's relation to the world (see pp. 18–20, above).

Through those who are the great knowers, the great artists, the great lovers, and above all through the great men of faith, new forms are constantly embodied within the world of our perception, forming the sphere of the interhuman, the human *cosmos* which guides our relation to things and persons, drawing it into the depths.[43] These basic relations are shown diagrammatically in Chart 2. But at this point in the text of *I and Thou* (§ 9) the full development of such themes is only hinted at in exceedingly cryptic statements. However, with the close of this section, the text moves from compact aphorisms to more diffuse statements. The basic themes have been enunciated; Buber now proceeds with their orchestration.

Particular Regions (§§ 10–12)

Relation to nature (§ 10). Meeting with the subhuman exercised a deep influence upon Martin Buber. Again and again he refers to his experience with a piece of mica or with an animal or

41. "Man and His Image Work," KM, p. 163.
42. "Replies," PMB, p. 689.
43. "Postscript," *I and Thou*, pp. 127–30.

a tree.[44] Here he treats of the latter relation in a compact description of the various approaches one might take to the tree. In logical form they are the following:

I. It-Relation
    A. Object of experience
        1. sensory
            a) individual
                i) static
                ii) dynamic
            b) species
        2. intellectual construction
            a) cluster of laws
                i) dynamic forces
                ii) static proportions
            b) numerical relations
    B. Object of use
II. Thou-Relation

Thus one might consider the tree as an object (an It) structured in terms of its relation to the subject, either as object of experience or as object of use (and the two are related). In the former case, the object is either sensory or intellectual. Classically, this distinction has been made in terms of the distinction between particularity and universality. Not so in Buber. An intellectual object for Buber is one which does not directly present itself to sense experience: it is a construction. The universality-particularity distinction applies to the object as present to the senses, depending upon whether we consider the tree in its individual appearance or as a representative of its species. In the former case, we can again consider the individual statically, as a picture with the fullness of its sense qualities, or dynamically, in terms of its basic vital movements as they manifest themselves to the senses. But in any case, the sense object is a consideration of the Other as it affects the percipient organism, as an impression (*Eindruck*).

For Buber the images of our perception are not in things, but

44. MICA: "Ueber Jakob Boehme," pp. 251–53; *Daniel*, p. 140; § 52. ANIMAL: "Dialogue," BMM, p. 23; § 52. TREE: "Ueber Jakob Boehme," pp. 251–53; WM, BMM, p. 178; *Daniel*, pp. 47 and 54; "Man and His Image Work," KM, p. 157.

only in the sphere of our relation to things. The green, the rough, the cool, the fragrant—all await the percipient senses in order to come into being as such. The senses likewise function as a filter, providing from many potential effects streaming from the environment only that which man needs for his biological adjustment. Animals dwell exclusively within this "functional circle." [45] But man, as creature of distance, existing "over-against" the world, is aware that "the being that is perceived . . . is not identical with the existing being with whom I have contact." This duality in man's relationship sets up a fruitful tension that can lead to a deeper relation.[46]

But one can likewise abstract from the unique presence and perceived form (*Diesmaligkeit,* "this-time-ness," and *Geformtheit,* "formed-ness") of the tree and consider it in terms of intellectual construction (*Vorstellung*) based ultimately on the a priori structures of space, time, and causality (see pp. 68–71, below). Then it appears as a cluster of law-governed relations: dynamic laws of the balance of forces, static laws of chemical proportion. It can even be considered in terms of pure numerical relations.[47]

In every instance, both in the regions of sense perception and of intellectual interpretation, the Other is definable only in terms of its reference back to the designations of the knowing subject as this subject's *object of experience.* In and through this objectification, the Other may be viewed simultaneously as object of my evaluation (*Stimmungswert*) or, as Buber will shortly speak of it, as *object of use* which follows upon the ordering of the data.[48]

In a radically different way, all the preceding may be gathered up indivisibly in the event whereby one is "bound up in relation," "seized by the power of exclusiveness," involved in a mutuality. But this only occurs through the meeting of man's

45. "Man and His Image Work," KM, pp. 154 ff.; "Distance and Relation," KM, pp. 60 ff.

46. "Bergson's Concept of Intuition," PW, p. 83.

47. Toward the end of his life Buber will backtrack on this analysis as it applies to mathematics. The substratum underlying the sense forms is comprehensible through mathematics ("Man and His Image Work," KM, p. 154). Mathematics is a relation to being itself (IMB, p. 48). If this is so, it may require a complete revision of his philosophy.

48. "Distance and Relation," KM, p. 65.

will and a gift (*Gnade*) that comes to us from the Other. (Here Buber introduces some of the basic characteristics of the Thou-relation which he will treat in somewhat more detailed fashion in §§ 13–21.) At the level of the Thou-relation, mere observation, which deals only with what we need from the world, is transcended in what Buber will later call "vision," which is a deepened perception, faithful not to appearance but to being.[49]

It has been suggested [50] that the grounds for Thou-relation to things of nature can be located in three logical options: (1) the tree has a "soul"; (2) the tree is part of an animated whole; (3) the tree is composed of animated individuals. Buber rejects this attempt as representing a position wherein he cannot find his own thought.[51] That does not mean that Buber's thought and this attempt at grounding are incompatible; it only means that Buber personally does not think in terms of the options presented.

One could, however, question whether these options are the only ones possible. Things may "say" something to us, and that saying may be grounded in a mode of being to whose basic structure we at present simply have no adequate access and about which we cannot even form meaningful theoretical options. This would seem to be Buber's position, since he presents this whole realm as "sunk in mystery." He asks us to "believe in the simple magic of life" (§ 19). Perhaps there are certain things that had better be let be—not forgotten, through lack of interest, but attended to in a mode which transcends conceptual mastery. To attain to a set of logical alternatives in this regard may give us a kind of pseudo-self-security which removes us from the attentiveness to life to which Buber recalls us.

Relation to men (§ 11). A human being also, insofar as he is an empirically observable entity, can be considered as an instance of a species within a network of relations and as himself composed of more elementary structures: a thing among things composed of things. Indeed, there is nothing essentially different between Buber's analysis of our relation to men in this section and his previous analysis of our relation with the subhuman, with this one exception: here examples of relation with the

49. "Man and His Image Work," KM, pp. 159 ff.
50. Charles Hartshorne, "Martin Buber's Metaphysics," PMB, pp. 55–56.
51. "Replies," PMB, p. 717.

forms of the spirit in works of art are brought forth to illuminate the human relation.

Encounter with a man is like encounter with the works of the spirit: with a poem, a piece of music, or a statue. All have elements of empirical structure which can be isolated, analyzed, and correlated. But the act by which this occurs is other than the act by which we are given over to the vision of total meaningfulness embodied in each of the empirical structures. Indeed, it seems to require a special effort to move from the vision to the analysis: the elements of structure must be "tugged and dragged until their unity has been scattered into these many pieces." The art relation seems to furnish a basic analogue of the Thou-relation.

This apparent reduction of human Thou-relations to relations with cultural works seems peculiar, since the prime analogate of the Thou-relation would seem to be the one whom man immediately addresses as Thou: his fellow man. The peculiarity increases when Buber proceeds to maintain that the human Thou need not even be aware of any Thou-saying to him, whereas he had just maintained (§ 10) that relation with things of nature is *mutual*. He will go on to say that mutuality is essential to all modes of relation (§§ 19–20) and will then explain that there is a mutuality involved in simply being, even without awareness.[52] It may be the case that Buber is basing himself upon the observation that since interhuman relations usually involve a great mixture of need-fulfillment and sham representations of Thou-relations which are really disguised forms of egoism,[53] and since relations with a work of art involve no exposure of our being to the danger of betrayal which all human relations involve, Thou-relations with works of art are more apt to occur. Hence Buber uses the latter to illumine the otherwise mixed interpersonal relations.

Buber then seemingly shifts attention from the human sphere and notes that, in all these regions of relation, when one steps outside the finite structures of man's objectification into relation, one steps beyond all limitation. Hence the transobjective relation of the Thou is a relation which spills over the limitations of empirical structures and gathers together the to-

52. "Postscript," *I and Thou*, p. 126.
53. "Dialogue," BMM, pp. 29–30.

tality in the light of the meaningfulness met with in the Other. It is in this dimension of transcendence that authentic prayer and sacrifice occur; it is here that a man breaks out of the network of necessary sequence ("causality") and the rule of fate woven about him by the workings of his own intelligence.[54] Man attains to his freedom simultaneously with his transcendence of an appearance-bound experience in meeting with the Other in his otherness. I become myself through my saying *Thou*.

Why do prayer and sacrifice and fate appear in this section on relation with men? Actually, the whole section is rather odd: relation with men is presented as no different from relation with nature and is illuminated by relation with the forms of the spirit. Now relation with the Transcendent in prayer and sacrifice and wrestling with fate appear almost as an appendage to this section. It might be suggested that it is precisely because of the centrality of man's meeting with *man* that all these other relations are dwelt upon here. Through meeting with man, the notion of a *cosmos,* a vision of the totality, takes shape in an individual [55]—a vision formed by generation upon generation of ancestors.[56] Through the progressive augmentation of the world of It as the spinning-out of man's constructions, the web of fate begins to tighten about the individual (§ 36). And it is together that men develop their prayer and sacrifice to the Eternal Thou (§ 61). "It is from one man to another that the heavenly bread of self-being is passed." [57]

Relation to the forms of the spirit (§ 12). The forms of the spirit appear in the areas of art, thought, and "activity" (*Handlung*). Here Buber treats of one of the areas: the prime analogate, *art*. Indeed, for Buber all the areas seem reducible to some form of art, i.e., to a creative activity of man. *Handlung* as the forming of one's life in terms of relation is indeed an art—the art of arts. And Buber sees even thinking as a kind of art when he compares philosophy with painting.[58]

In any of these cases it is not a matter of a subjective projection upon the objective world [59] but of a *Gestalt* which

54. See § 36 and "With a Monist," PW, pp. 26–27.
55. "What Is Common to All," KM, p. 91.
56. "Man and His Image Work," KM, pp. 160–61.
57. "Distance and Relation," KM, p. 71.
58. "Bergson's Concept of Intuition," PW, p. 84; § 32.
59. "Man and His Image Work," KM, p. 161.

meets man and urges him to give it embodiment in a work. As he will later express it, art is "the realm of the 'between' which has become form," the meeting between the *substantia humana* and the *substantia rerum*.[60] But because these meetings occur in the Between, the work of art "arises from this world's meeting with the other."[61] This is the realm of the spirit which encompasses nature (§ 26), the realm pointing to the transcendent mystery of being.[62] As such, the form is not initially there in an empirically verifiable sense. But a call is given for embodiment whereby the form is led over into the empirically verifiable world in word and work,[63] in those sense forms whereby man comes to communicate meaning. Spirit is then housed in matter: the substance of this world is given increase. But with embodiment goes objectification, and with objectification the danger of becoming mere It. The work of art becomes a cultural object open to the critics; the text becomes an object of scholarly research; the life of a man who has been formed in the spirit becomes a set of data for biographers (§ 32). What has passed out of the object is the vision, the inspiration. But the embodiment has secured the vision: the Thou is contained within the chrysalis of objectification, waiting to be brought forth through personal response evoked anew from the depths.[64] Original word and work are the creative man's contribution to the community.

In dealing with relation to nature, Buber listed several characteristics of relation: the meeting of will and grace, exclusiveness, mutuality, and totalization. Here he adds presentness. Will and grace are evident in the fact that the form must initially present itself and that man must be disposed for the meeting. This involves a mutuality of effects where the form takes hold of a man and he responds in the work. The notion of presence, which is central, is left here without explanation, but it will be taken up shortly. Exclusiveness appears as a special characteristic of relation at this level. A special demand is placed upon the one who encounters a form that has not yet been embodied: a

60. "Distance and Relation," KM, p. 66; "Man and His Image Work," p. 165.
61. "Postscript," *I and Thou*, p. 129.
62. WM, BMM, p. 177.
63. "Postscript," *I and Thou*, p. 130.
64. § 22. See Diamond (*Martin Buber*, pp. 24–26) for a fine description of how this may occur in music.

demand to lay aside all other possibilities and give himself up to the work of embodying the form.[65]

LEADING CHARACTERISTICS OF THE THOU-MEETING (§§ 13–21)

HAVING LAID DOWN the basic notions of the text and having then briefly discussed the three regions of relation, Buber now moves into a discussion of some of the leading characteristics of the Thou-relation: totalization (§ 13), the coming-together of will and grace (§ 14), immediacy (§§ 15–18), and mutuality (§§ 19–21).

Totalization (§ 13)

In the Thou-relation an indistinguishable fusing of all characteristics takes place—what we are here calling "totalization." Though there may be any number of objectifiable elements involved in the encounter (cf. § 10), the Thou itself stands "beyond" any and all of these elements as the source of their unity. But to meet that unity is to meet "in principle" all the multiplicity that flows from it. However, the "standing-beyond" and the "in principle" are not to be taken as referring to a metaphysical or logical substratum from which all the characteristics are deducible. Buber is strictly descriptive here. Meeting is a lived relation of whole to whole, and it requires an entirely different act of attentiveness to sort out objectifiable characteristics from the meeting. But because these characteristics have been sorted out of the original meeting, they are capable of being led back to the unity involved, even though this occurs only with difficulty. We are ultimately dealing here with what cannot be classified as such, namely with "concretion itself" [66]—the *con-crescens*, the growing-together into unity of all classifiable elements.

The kind of knowledge involved here is an entirely different sort from the kind that operates within the subject-object relation: it is the kind involved when Adam "knew" Eve.[67] Buber will

65. "What Is Common to All," KM, p. 102.
66. "Dialogue," BMM, p. 16.
67. "Philosophische und religiöse Weltanschauung," *Nachlese*, p. 128.

call this "seeing the whole" (§ 21) or "synthesizing apperception," [68] which is a knowing of uniqueness and thus an exclusive type of knowing (cf. §§ 10, 12, 19, 27). It forms the necessary prerequisite for saying *Thou*. This sort of knowing in turn presupposes the coming-together of two factors—a coming-together which constitutes the second characteristic of the Thou-relation.

The Coming-Together of Will and Grace (§ 14)

If meeting is to occur, one's intention and consequent preparation must surely be involved. Buber will talk of "imagining the real" (*Realphantasie*) [69] and of "inclusion" of the Other [70] as necessary psychological prerequisites, drawing us out of mere subjective preoccupation. One must become the kind of person who can enter into relation; but this is only a prerequisite. Ultimately, the Thou has to give itself. Some sort of grace is involved. This is not simply a matter of another person consciously entering into friendship; in that case, the "grace" factor becomes more intelligible (though even here friendship as much "happens" as it is chosen). The gift-character is likewise the case in meeting with things of nature, with the forms of the spirit, and with other persons *as natures* (i.e., apart from their conscious intention) (see comments on § 10, above, pp. 45 ff.). Buber strongly resists attempts at psychologizing such relations, reducing them merely to the subject's state of mind; the Other has a more than passive role to play.[71] Activity and passivity are united in the single act in which one gives and receives the Thou.[72] All particular acts and faculties are suspended, so that one appears to be doing nothing; [73] and yet the central act of one's being is performed in saying *Thou*, for here alone does one attain to wholeness. Since the saying is not possible at all with-

68. "Distance and Relation," KM, p. 62.
69. "Elements of the Interhuman," KM, pp. 80–81.
70. "Education," BMM, p. 97.
71. "With a Monist," PW, p. 27.
72. Smith's translation of *Passion* here as "suffering" makes little sense. "Passivity" is clearly the correct translation, as is indicated by the whole context.
73. "The Teaching of the Tao," PW, pp. 53–55; § 46.

out the Other's offering itself, the Between's actualization does not simply depend upon my attitude.[74] In actuality the I attains its wholeness only through the Other, as a gift from the Other (or perhaps from Someone beyond the Other Who beckons to us through the Between) (cf. § 46). One's life totality is possible only through the Other's cooperation. "All real living is meeting."

Immediacy (Unmittelbarkeit) (§§ 15–18)

Through reflection we come to mediate our relation to the Other by linking it to similar things in the *past* or by fitting it into our *future* projects—either our own deliberately calculated aims (*Zweck*), the cravings of our nature (*Gier*), or simply our speculative anticipations (*Vorwegnahme*) of the future possibilities of things (§ 15). We may also attempt to transcend these temporal relations by referring the Other to a system of *transtemporal* ideas (§ 18). But all this is objectification and hence fundamentally mirrors back the structures of the knowing-desiring subject. Real meeting involves a transcendence of all such subjective mediation to arrive at authentic *immediacy*. Hence the crucial distinction for Buber is between *Gegenstand* and *Gegenwart;* between the opposite (*Gegen*), which stands (*steht*) in indifference to be manipulated by man, and that which awaits (*wartet*) man's response; between *object* and *presence*.[75]

To dwell in objectification is to reduce the present to the past in the sense that the uniqueness we meet is considered only in terms of what it has in common with others we have encountered: the Other becomes object of (organized) *experience*. Future anticipation reduces the Other to an object of *use*, which is the corollary of the organization of experience. As such this future projection is simply another mode of dwelling in the past, for the Other is considered in terms of schemata that have already been disclosed.[76] Objects are past; only relation is present (§ 17).

Note here that it is not a question of removing all objectification but of removing the mediatory status that objectification

74. James Brown interprets Buber this way (*Kierkegaard, Heidegger, Buber and Barth* [New York: Collier, 1962], p. 108).

75. See Theunissen, "Bubers negative Ontologie," pp. 322–23.

76. See Friedman, *Life*, pp. 168–69.

tends to bring about.[77] There is a tendency to focus attention not upon the being that is present but upon the categories within which it fits. Many things Buber says leave the impression that he is constantly attacking objective knowing, but he is merely trying to offset a habit long ingrained in Western man.[78] As Buber sees it, objectification has an important role to play, not only in the development of the practical world, but in developing the Thou-relation itself. The purpose of objectification is the enlargement for the I of the being encountered so as to provoke a more profound meeting. To achieve that, the objective elements must be brought back to unity in encounter (cf. § 28). But this is where the difficulty lies: the way back from object to presence is increasingly obscured. With the hardening of our categories of interpretation and goal-projection, wonder disappears from life; we become "adult," and the world becomes familiar, routine. We lose the capacity to sense the depth hidden within the simple *presence* of things; real living disappears. And when living mutuality vanishes, then mistrust, curiosity, and routine step in to establish the fundamental modes of relation to others.[79] With the disappearance of relation, religion likewise disappears, for the true name for religion, according to Buber, is *presentness*.[80]

If we ponder a moment the notion of presence, we may see a bit more clearly what Buber is about here. As we reflect upon the conscious situation, we see ourselves "here," facing objects "there." A careful inspection of the objects reveals more and more elements within the initial experience. An introspective act of attention yields more and more complex structures involved in our modes of dealing with objects. But what escapes such acts of attentiveness is presence: the original bond *between* subject and objects (which indeed is *always* there as the ground of the mutuality involved). Presence is the mutual givenness of subject and object, the primary togetherness which antedates their separation through reflection. This is why Buber sees (and will shortly consider) children and primitives as clear instances of

77. Brown (*Kierkegaard,* pp. 104–5) sees the distinction here as one between *presence* and *re-presentation,* i.e., between real presence and the surrogate presence of a being in the mind.

78. "Replies," PMB, p. 704.

79. "Gemeinschaft und Umwelt," *Nachlese,* p. 85.

80. "The Baal-Shem-Tov's Instruction in Intercourse with God," HMM, p. 181.

the life of relation (cf. §§ 23–27). But presence is likewise capable of intensification, and it is precisely in authentically religious people that the deepening of presence is realized. The saint lives in the presence of God in such a way that each thing becomes a theophany, a manifestation of a Presence that appears in and through all other presences.

Now, our view of presence determines our view of time. With Bergson, Buber develops two modes of time: what Buber calls cosmological time and anthropological time [81] and what Bergson calls abstract and concrete time. In abstract, quantitative time the present is only the discrete, extensionless point separating past from future, whereas concrete, qualitative time is the durational flow of real events.[82] Abstract time is really timeless time, time viewed in terms of space as a row of qualitatively undifferentiated points laid out in the present. Concrete time is qualitatively articulated and involved in an attention to what unfolds in the present. This present is the sustained and deepening *presence* of the Thou to the I (§ 17).

There are actually two components to this presence. Buber will later emphasize the distinction between relation (*Beziehung*) and meeting (*Begegnung*). The latter suggests the fleeting character involved in the actual realization of the Thou-relation; the former is of wider extension, including the latent state of openness, preparedness, commitment.[83]

The tension between presence and object cannot be sublated by appeal to a transtemporal world of Ideas (§ 18). For one thing, Buber rejects such a realm—and for that commentators have seen him as a nominalist.[84] At least it is clear that he is not an extreme realist on the question of universals. For Buber, ideas originate out of meeting and gradually attain expression and refinement through removal from the moment of meeting, becoming welded into a system of related ideas that stand apart from immediate presence.[85] But when they reach that stage, they

81. WM, BMM, p. 140.
82. Henri Bergson, *Time and Free Will*, trans. F. L. Pogson (London: Allen & Unwin, 1950), pp. 90–91 and *passim*.
83. "Replies," PMB, pp. 705, 712.
84. Kohn, *Martin Buber*, p. 26; Maringer, *Martin Bubers Metaphysik*, p. 26. For Buber's rejection of the transtemporal realm of ideas see "Postscript," *I and Thou*, p. 129.
85. "Dialogue," BMM, p. 27; § 32.

enter the world of orientation, the world of It, and *as such* cannot become presentness for us (§ 46). It takes a great man indeed to bring them down from the heaven of abstraction "to the earth of bodily meetings," though it is possible.[86]

Conceptual system is necessary to give structure to human life. And in this role the thinker must be carefully attentive to the "inner court," "the basic relation in face of which he has to answer for his insight." He addresses something more than himself.[87] And yet the conceptual system is merely the skeletal structure of life, not its vitality.[88] Furthermore, even as general ideas enter into the structure of a system, they are always relative to the conceptual and experiential material available in the age within which the thinker operates.[89] Conceptual knowledge must be constantly recast in the light of an attentiveness to the changing situation within which man dwells.[90] Even though the logical unfolding of an idea demands that the thinker attend to the other-than-self involved in the logical relations, purely logical thinking must always be subordinated to that basic dialogical thinking which needs the unpredictable manifestation of the Other.[91] As Buber sees it, the difference here

is by no means that between the "rational" and the "irrational," but that between the reason that detaches itself from the other forces of the human person and declares itself to be the sovereign and the reason that forms a part of the wholeness and unity of the human person and works, serves, and expresses itself within this wholeness and unity.[92]

86. IMB, p. 57 and pp. 46–47.
87. "Dialogue," BMM, p. 26. Hence the inadequacy of Robert Gotshalk's criticism that Buber has failed to extend the notion of responsibility to objective thinking ("Buber's Conception of Responsibility," *Journal of Existentialism*, VI, No. 21 [1965], 1–8). Buber later refines his position further: Man is never responsible to ideas *as such* but always to a "living personal court. . . . I do not hold the idea of eternal peace to be fictitious, but he who says to me that he is responsible to it, is an enthusiast or a phrase-monger" ("Replies," PMB, p. 698).
88. IMB, p. 67.
89. "Zur Situation der Philosophie," *Nachlese*, pp. 136–38.
90. IMB, p. 17.
91. Maringer, *Martin Bubers Metaphysik*, p. 109.
92. "Replies," PMB, p. 710.

By entering into the word of living dialogue, monological thought breaks open and grows. "In thought reason is dominant, in the word it is life."[93]

When Buber comes down to his final stand, even though he often seems to place relation to nature and to the forms of the spirit on a par with relation to men, it is only in the realm of the *Zwischenmenschlichen* that ideas are "raised to being itself."[94] Logical thought itself not only demands a basis in the situation where meeting occurs, but it calls out for complementarity and challenge by another human being.[95] Here as elsewhere, ultimately it is the mode of saying rather than what is said that counts;[96] content is always subordinated to the mode of presence,[97] I-It to I-Thou, for technical dialogue is not yet I-Thou.[98]

There are a number of moments to be described in this whole process of relating presence and objectification. First there is the original mutual presence without the reflective break of subject and object (cf. § 24). Second, there is the establishment of a separate realm of abstract ideas which are considered in themselves and without direct reference to individuals. Third, there is the establishment of mediation within the immediacy of our relation to things, which diminishes presence by the gradual shift of attention within the polar relation with the Other to the self-reflective categories of interpretation and use (cf. § 24). Fourth, there is the fusing of all mediation within immediacy (§ 10), the totalization through which presence deepens.[99]

Underlying the third movement is a tendency toward real value-nihilism in that the Other-as-interpreted is, for Buber, the

93. Biser, "Martin Buber," p. 109a.
94. "What Is Common to All," KM, p. 107.
95. "Dialogue," BMM, p. 27.
96. IMB, pp. 33–34.
97. Anzenbacher, *Die Philosophie*, p. 56.
98. Buber's notion of dialogue cuts across I-Thou and I-It. There are two modes of dialogue: the "genuine" dialogue of the I-Thou relation, which is the deepening of mutual presence, and technical dialogue, which aims at objective understanding only. The latter would be divisible into the logical, which unfolds in itself, and that which—whatever it may be termed—seeks the human Other for confirmation and/or opposition. Opposed to both of these is monological thinking, which is sheer subjectivism and which often disguises itself as dialogue ("Dialogue," BMM, pp. 19–20).
99. "Distance and Relation," KM, p. 64.

Other as reflecting my (speculative or practical) needs. From this point of view, the Other appears as *in itself* value-neutral and hence valueless. Authentic value for Buber lies in relation to the *total* otherness of the Other as value-in-itself. And this is found in presence. Dwelling in the third movement, one may gradually come to sense, in a prereflective way, the nihilism underlying the subjectively restructured life world and seek refuge in the realm of abstraction as pure value.[100] Like Plato, he may dwell in the realm of the pure ought; [101] or like the mystics he may flee to the aloneness of Primal Being. In either case the immediate and everyday presence to things is left aside, and life becomes split into the special exalted hours of illumination and the "fallen" days and months and years of ordinary life. Like the Stoics, he may seek to serve "Humanity"; [102] but if Humanity is not present in the bodiliness of one who meets me here and now, life is betrayed. Real living is meeting within deepening presence.

Mutuality (§§ 19–21)

Will and grace provide the necessary preconditions for meeting. What follows from it is a mutuality of effects. "My Thou affects me, as I affect it" (§ 20). Buber now treats, in turn, the effect of the I upon the Thou (§ 19) and then (briefly) the effect of the Thou upon the I (§ 20). A questioner breaks into the text at this point and touches off a brief aside on love (§ 21).

Forms of the spirit. Though an effect upon the Thou occurs in all three of the regions of relation, it is most evident in the region of the forms of the spirit. This is especially true in art, where the form met is drawn out of the spaceless, timeless present into the spatiotemporal world through the creative activity of the artist. It enters the common world of men as an It which can become Thou for others.

Men. In the case of relation with men, the effect upon the Thou is misunderstood if one thinks in terms of response to

100. "Teaching and Deed," IW, p. 141. See also §§ 42–43.
101. See EG, p. 102, for Buber's coupling of Plato's Good and the Ought. See "Plato and Isaiah," IW, pp. 103–12 for an interesting comparison of Greek vision with Hebrew vision.
102. "Society and the State," PW, pp. 165–66.

the Thou as a matter of feeling. Feeling is something that occurs *within* man as a psychological phenomenon.[103] Love as the full realization of the Thou-relation is concerned with meeting and thus stands beyond the phenomena, whether these are physical or psychological. Love is the supreme articulation of the Between. Now, the Between is the Word (*Wort*); taking one's stand in the Word furnishes the basis for response (*Antwort*) to the Thou (cf. § 32); and it is only in terms of actual response that authentic responsibility (*Verantwortung*) occurs.[104] And precisely such responsibility is love (§ 19). In the total response of meeting, where will and grace find each other, all *real* effectiveness occurs: helping, healing, educating, raising up, saving. Outside of such a total act of authentic responsibility, none of these means of aiding ultimately aids the person. Without full responsiveness one affects the other only partially and superficially.[105]

Love in its authentic sense is the realization of relation and thus presupposes the totalization of vision, "seeing the whole." And to the extent that it does not see the whole, to the extent that it is "blind," love is not love, not a form of authentic dialogue, but one or the other form of monologue where the Other is a mirror of one's own self-interest.[106] And yet seeing the whole is not yet love, for love presupposes the *affirmation* of the being one sees. One may see the whole and not be able to say *Thou* (§ 21). And again, one may not be able to see the whole of the human Other as human through deception or withholding on the part of that Other.[107] But if the whole is seen and love is eventually to blossom, one must stand in the openness of authentic dialogue, prepared to receive what comes from the other side. However, such preparedness involves exposure to the risk of being hurt by what comes from the Other. Some may retreat

103. Hence Agus (*Modern Philosophies*, p. 248) is once more off the mark, as he identifies the Thou-relation with feeling and then claims that there is no means of distinguishing authentic relation from fanaticism since in both cases the self *feels* sure of his authenticity.

104. "Dialogue," BMM, p. 16.

105. See "Healing through Meeting," PW, pp. 93–97; "Education," BMM, pp. 83–103; "The Education of Character," BMM, pp. 104–17; "Spirit and Body of the Hasidic Movement," OMH, pp. 141 ff.

106. "Dialogue," BMM, pp. 28–30.

107. "Elements of the Interhuman," KM, pp. 74–75.

from this risk by mere solicitude, which is concern without exposure and thus not full mutuality, for one does not expect or allow anything from the other side.[108]

The subhuman. As far as relation to the subhuman is concerned, Buber goes no further in his analysis. Mutuality here remains sunk in mystery, but it is real for the one who really meets the things of nature (§ 19). One's response to nature effects something profound in it (§ 55). Behind this conviction lies one of the core experiences of the Hasidim: that each least thing has a *Gestalt* within it which is a divine spark that belongs to the root of *man's* soul. These sparks are the exiled glory of God, His *Shekinah.* Man is a creature deeply embedded in the total cosmos. As such, his acts have cosmic repercussions. Through man's act of turning with his whole being to things, he releases the sparks and allows God's glory to dwell in the world. "Man is commissioned and summoned as a cosmic mediator to awaken a holy reality in things through holy contact with them." [109]

If the self affects the Other, the Other likewise has its effect upon the self, for one's self-being is not one's own doing only; it is likewise the gift of the Other. Each thing to which one offers oneself gives in its turn to the self (§ 20). But especially is this true in the case of man with man: "It is from one man to another that the heavenly bread of self-being is passed." [110]

FROM THOU TO IT (§§ 22–27)

General Considerations (§ 22)

EVERY THOU ENCOUNTERED in immediacy, totalization, responsibility, affirmation, and mutuality inevitably becomes an It, a thing among things. The realization of the work

108. WM, BMM, p. 170. This is one of Buber's chief criticisms against Heidegger.
109. HMM, p. 33. See also "The Baal-Shem-Tov's Instruction," HMM, pp. 187–89; "The Beginnings," OMH, p. 50; "The Foundation Stone," OMH, p. 83; "Spirit and Body," OMH, pp. 117 ff. Behind this conception lies the Kabbalah, and behind the Kabbalah lie both Neoplatonism and the Old Testament, which the Kabbalist doctrine attempted to synthesize.
110. "Distance and Relation," KM, p. 71.

of art means the loss of the immediate encounter with the form embodied in it; contemplation of the subhuman ends up in description, analysis, classification, and systematization; love leads to an objectification of the beloved. But in all this there is the alternation of the actual and the latent: once achieved, relation is recognized as that which is hidden within the Thou-become-It, and from time to time it can be actualized—provided one persists in faithful openness. The situation of thinghood envelops the Thou as a chrysalis envelops the butterfly. But in being reduced to this state, the It is located as something that can become Thou for others. Hence the It-world has a function to play that is essential. Relation, however, is first; out of relation all thinglike structures emerge to people man's world. This development can be traced in the history of the race as well as in the growth of individuals.

Historical Development from Thou to It (§§ 23–27)

Primitives (§§ 23–26). Primitive peoples live a life highly charged with presence within a narrow circle of object structures. "Not things but situations are primary." [111] This is indicated by the linguistic usage of primitives, which is filled with words expressive of presence. The original situation is one of living experience (*Erlebnis*) in relation to the fleeting incidents and the more enduring situations which stand over against the primitive man. Out of these original encounters emerge such early concepts as *Mana,* as effective power met with in certain circumstances. This is the initial abstraction of the primitive man; it has nothing at all to do with the "supernatural" and yet is worlds apart from the scientific notion of causality as an unbroken chain of events. *Mana* is an unpredictable (but nonetheless classifiable) bursting-forth of power, the power of the Thou. As the memory learns to put the powerful relational events into order and *Mana* becomes an ordered series of events, the less common and shifting Thou retires and the perduring I emerges for the first time (§ 23). Such a situation creates a state of crisis for the primitive, who is a naïve pansacramentalist. He discovers the region of the not-holy, which progressively enlarges itself. [112]

111. "The Word That Is Spoken," KM, p. 116.
112. "Symbolic and Sacramental Existence," OMH, p. 167.

The world of It has started on its historical way, and with it goes the separated I.

Buber distinguishes a number of stages in which this emergence occurs. First is the original relational event, where the I is included only implicitly. Here the simultaneous eruption of the I and the manifest Other occurs spontaneously with, and defines, the emergence of man. Second, the body as bearer of its perceptions is separated out from the environment: man apparently becomes aware of his enduring bodily center as a distinct entity in the environment,[113] but he is not yet aware of his awareness. Third, with the latter occurrence, i.e., with the awareness of awareness, the I of the relational event is awakened to its own distinctness as consciousness: for the first time, man really says and means "I." And once the I emerges in fuller self-consciousness, the whole of the world can be seen as standing over against him as his object (§ 24). Now, for the first time, spirit, which always surrounds nature, is manifest in time and inaugurates the history of man as he emerges from mere nature. Spirit itself is the Between, the Word present in the natural relational event of primitive man but not yet manifest. When man becomes capable of creative response in objective form, spirit is *manifest* in man (cf. § 32), and this occurs through the emergence of the separated I. From this point of view it *appears* as though spirit emerges from nature in man; actually it is spirit that makes the emergence possible. "Spirit appears in time as a product—even as a by-product of nature, yet it is in spirit that nature is timelessly enveloped" (§ 25).[114]

This emergence is a mixed blessing for man. Through the development of the world of It which the separation of the I introduces, the spiritual substance of man begins to grow; but the danger of the alienation of spirit from life is immanent. However, as the alienation grows more oppressive, turning back

113. "Das Judentum und die Juden," *Reden*, JSJ, p. 12.

114. Brown (*Kierkegaard*, p. 106) sees this passage as an indication of a metaphysical assumption. Buber would claim that it bears witness to experience which involves a transtemporal reference ("Aus einer philosophischer Rechenschaft," W I, pp. 1113–14). It is precisely in the context of the discussion of spirit that Buber sees metaphysical assumptions as poisoning the wells of experience (WM, BMM, pp. 182 ff.). But one has to admit that the move from experience of man's transcendent reference to the claim that spirit timelessly envelops nature is a rather long leap.

to relation becomes more profound (cf. § 61). Man matures through becoming, introduced by the world of It; he arrives at being through turning back with his increased substance to the Source (cf. § 55).

I-Thou and I-It emerge out of the dualism of elements inherent in creation itself. This dualism is given many names in different cultures: matter and form, being and becoming, active and passive, male and female, positive and negative.[115] All point to a fundamental polarity in which the two aspects complement each other in their opposition to form a relational unity. This polarity-in-unity manifests itself likewise in the life of the child, where the growth of the two primary words out of the structures of nature can be traced.

The development of the child (§ 27). This section contains a number of positions that are central to the foundations of Buber's thought. Our analysis will focus on two key notions: (1) the cosmic-metacosmic origin of man and (2) the undivided primal world that precedes form.

For Buber, man is a creature of dual origin: he is brought forth from below and sent from above,[116] emergent from the cosmos and graced with a metacosmic principle. The metacosmic principle is spirit as relation between man and that which transcends the world, as relation to the Creator.[117] This relation provides the original distance (*Urdistanz*) from the things of the world which grounds the revelation of the otherness of the Other, for full otherness is revealable only to one who is fully other.[118] One who merely springs from below, from the cosmos, is part of the cosmic process and as such is not wholly other.[119] Relation to transcendence, participation in infinity, is

115. *Daniel*, p. 136.
116. EG, p. 127.
117. "Das Unbewusste," *Nachlese*, p. 151; "The Faith of Judaism," IW, p. 27; "The Power of the Spirit," IW, p. 180.
118. "Distance and Relation," KM, p. 60; "What Is Common to All," KM, p. 96.
119. This interpretation dissolves Nathan Rotenstreich's difficulty, for he sees the notion of *Urdistanz* as destroying Buber's fundamental position on the primacy of relation ("Some Problems in Buber's Dialogical Philosophy," *Philosophy Today*, III, No. 3 [1959], 160). Again, contrary to Rotenstreich (pp. 159–60) and Anzen-

what makes knowledge possible as the manifestation of other-ness.[120]

Yet man is no centaur; he is man through and through, a unitary entity.[121] The cosmic and metacosmic principles unite in the unconscious, which for Buber is the fundamental being of man,[122] "the undivided primal world which precedes form" (§ 27). Notice that the unconscious is a *world* and thus seemingly involves more than the individual. Perhaps this is why Buber says that in his mother's womb a man knows the universe and that (therefore) he rests not only in the biological womb but also in the Womb of the Great Mother, the Unconscious. Indeed, for Buber this is what it means to have a soul: to be related to the world. "Soul is to be understood in terms of the relation between man and world," just as "spirit is to be understood in terms of the relation between man and that which is not world, between man and being." [123] It is through the presence of spirit as relation to Transcendence that this world relation, which is soul, not only *is* but is *manifest*. Through the development of spirit, the world of form emerges in two sets of phenomena: the psychological and the physical. The original distance of man reveals both the Other and man's perceptions of the Other.[124]

The dissociation of these two sets of phenomena is the only way in which the individual can become manifest to himself, and thus mind-body dualism is actually a polarity established within the unity of man's being for the purpose of making conscious, and thus raising to the level of spirit, that very unity.[125] Dualism is "the biography of psycho-physical unity." [126] The origi-

---

bacher (*Die Philosophie*, pp. 41, 51, 79), *Urdistanz* is *not* a reflective attitude but a grounding structure of human nature ("Replies," PMB, p. 695).

120. WM, BMM, p. 121.

121. *Ibid.*, p. 160.

122. "Das Unbewusste," *Nachlese*, p. 162; "Healing through Meeting," PW, p. 94.

123. "Von der Verseelung der Welt," *Nachlese*, p. 151. Translation mine.

124. "Distance and Relation," KM, pp. 59 ff.

125. "The Power of the Spirit," IW, p. 175.

126. ". . . Die Biographie der Leib-Seele-Einheit" ("Das Unbewusste," *Nachlese*, p. 186). This seems to be that primordial polarity which Buber sees as reaching a peculiar state of awareness in the Jewish people (see pp. 13–15, above).

nal unity lies in the unconscious, which is neither psychological nor physical but is the unitary ground of both phenomena. But the unconscious, in turn, does not lie *within* the self.[127] To be is to be related: everything in the world is being-with-others.[128] One's self-unity originally does not belong to oneself but is a function of relation to the Other; the full development of this unity at the conscious level is likewise a gift of the Other.[129] In the attainment of the spiritualization (i.e., the making-conscious) of one's unity, the unconscious has a basic role to play. Since meeting in its highest form is the relation of undivided to undivided,[130] it is a relation poles removed from that of the separated I viewing its objects. Soul and body enter into the relation together as the continuity between the unconscious and the conscious is brought to light.

The association of becoming whole through meeting specifies what is meant by that region of life in relation to the forms of the spirit which Buber called *Handlung* or "pure effective action" (§ 32; cf. § 9), where the form developed is the structure of one's own life. And the association of meeting with the unconscious likewise explains the peculiar use of the term *traumhaft* (dreaming) in § 28, where it appears in place of *handelnd* (acting) in the constantly appearing trinity of expressions dealing with the forms of the spirit. The *bildend, denkend,* and *handelnd* of § 9 become, in § 28, modes of acting characterized as *traumhaft, bildhaft,* and *gedankenhaft*. Becoming whole through meeting is so far from calculative, purposeful consciousness that Buber relates it to the state of dreaming and thus to close association with the unconscious, although I-Thou is a more intensive mode of awareness.[131]

Out of this dreamlike state, which does not obey the laws of objective consciousness, the great myths of the ages arise. In these myths man is seen as coming out of the Great Mother, who represents the underlying continuity of the living. Not only is the child in physical continuity with his biological mother; he is also in unconscious "beingly" continuity with the cosmos. What is

127. "Das Unbewusste," *Nachlese,* p. 164.
128. *Begegnung,* p. 15.
129. See pp. 89–90, below, on unity achieved in isolation. This, however, is not full unity—not the unity of *life*.
130. "Das Unbewusste," *Nachlese,* p. 182.
131. IMB, p. 39.

involved here is not only the world of the individual; in some way the world totality is also involved. To have a soul is precisely to be related to this totality.

But what is that relation? Buber does not explain it in detail. The Renaissance notion of the microcosm, which he spoke of in his first philosophic essay, seems to be akin to it. This notion involves not simply a mirroring of the universe from the perspective of an individual entity that is self-contained but implies rather a mutual inclusion. In each man the world comes into being all over again. This would ground Buber's conviction as to the cosmic character of man's act of turning to the Source through authentic meeting. Man and world in some way mutually include each other. One comes to one's own distinctness to the extent to which one makes that cosmic relation manifest.

The problem here is one of the most basic problems in philosophy: What do we mean by a unit of being? Logically we can distinguish four options, which are not necessarily mutually exclusive:

1. The unit of being is the ultimate particle composing the things of experience (Democritean atomism).
2. The unit of being lies in the individuals we encounter (Aristotelian substantialism).
3. The unit of being is the totality (a spectrum of positions from Parmenidean absolute monism to Whiteheadian organicism).
4. The unit of being lies in a transcendent principle within which all is rooted (Plotinian participationism).

Buber's position would be a variant of the third option. One's own distinctness from the world totality emerges with the progressively deepening awareness of one's identity with it. This is the paradox of awareness itself: that the mind exists in itself to the extent that it exists outside itself with the Other. But to be with the Other in the cognitive mode is to be aware of otherness and hence to ground the awareness of one's own distinctness. Awareness is an identity-in-difference.

Man's continuities with his mother and with the Great Mother are mere natural connections: each is a unity without differentiation and thus without awareness, a unity within the cosmos and not in relation to that which transcends the cosmos. The child emerges suddenly from the womb of its mother, but a long process of maturation must take place before the child gains sufficient distance to separate itself from the Great Mother. The maturation of the child consists in gradually learning to substitute a spiritual connection for the natural connection, which he gradually loses (§ 27). Note again, by "spiritual" Buber here means a totalization in consciousness of all man's capacities, powers, qualities, and urges,[132] a totalization which is possible only through meeting. Maturation is a bipolar process in which the Thou is enriched (at least potentially) through objectification (cf. § 28) and the I is enriched through a reflective development of subjectivity which does not lose touch with its relatedness (cf. § 39). For Buber the drive for this spiritual relation is an a priori structure (which he calls the "inborn Thou")[133] that has its roots in the original natural connection of bodily and unconscious continuity. Spirit furnishes the original distance, which is awakened through bodily separation from the mother. This distance sets off the world from the self, and the a priori drive moves the child to reach out for the Other. Through meeting, forms of perception arise, and the child is enabled to say *Thou* to what arises from this meeting.

Thou and It (§ 28)

As encounters come and go, the self gradually grows to an increased but prereflective awareness of its own enduring "this side" of the relational events. But there comes a time when the self turns back upon itself and develops a reflective awareness of its own distance from the world. The separated *cogito* makes its appearance [134] as the intellect severed from life which can now begin its objective conquest of the world. No longer defined by the whole relation of the undivided self to the undivided Other, the self as intellect is defined solely by its function of separating and arranging things. The I-It relation can now emerge as persistence in the original distance from things reflectively uncovered.[135]

132. "The Power of the Spirit," IW, p. 175.
133. John Baillie's interpretation of this as an innate idea of otherness chronologically prior to encounter is, I think, mistaken (*Our Knowledge of God* [New York: Scribner's, 1939], p. 213).
134. EG, pp. 39–40.
135. "Distance and Relation," KM, p. 64.

In his separation from things, man now directs his attention away from the unity of the individual to the various characteristics that are gathered up in a thing. He sets off part from part in space, and event from event in time, binding them all together in a causal chain. An ordered world arises, a world of separated entities extrinsically related in a necessary way.

In what way is the movement made from the individual to the totality? In a later work Buber conjoins the coming-into-being of a human world with the setting-up of an independent opposite.[136] Since man is a being wholly other than the entities in nature in view of his a priori transcendence toward the Transcendent, the *whole* of nature stands over against him. For Buber it is this original relation to wholeness that grounds our relation to the wholeness of the individual.[137] But a priori relation to the Transcendent merely *grounds* relation to the wholeness of the individual. It is only in actual fulfilled relation to the individual that a genuine conception of wholeness arises—i.e., one which is not a mere sum of parts.

Relation is chronologically first—as far as conscious life is concerned; it is grounded in the a priori relation to the Transcendent. As one reflectively uncovers the distance involved in relation, the independent I emerges and, along with it, an objective world. The shadow-image of authentic unity, secured in relation and grounded in the a priori structure of spirit, remains in the detached I, which can now develop a surrogate unity in an objectively ordered view of the totality composed of mutually external parts. But this ordered world is not the ordering of the world.[138] Like Bergson, Buber sees that the ordered world is only the transcription of the past unfolding of the real world into static terms, just as a musical score is a mere dry transcription, self-contained, completed, of that which is essentially dynamic and qualitatively differentiated: the musical performance itself. On the score each note is separated, one from another; in the performance, each blends with all the rest. Were we to concentrate upon the individual note, the rest would appear as back-

136. *Ibid.*, pp. 59–70, esp. 61–63.

137. ". . . The single being has received the character of wholeness and the unity which are perceived in it from the wholeness and unity perceived in the world" (*ibid.*, p. 63).

138. *Weltordnung.* This suggests a processive situation, whereas Smith's translation as "world-order" is just confusing (Smith, p. 31).

ground but not as separating boundary; there is complementarity, not separation.[139] So with the Thou-relation and the world that opens up through it—except that the musical performance is predictable in its unfolding, whereas the manifestations of the Thou are unpredictable.

When the separated I arises, spirit, too, emerges in its distinctness, and the urge to create unfolds in man. The forms of the spirit can now address him and demand embodiment. Man responds in religious myth-making (*traumhaft*) or in artistic fabrication (*bildhaft*) or in thought-creation (*gedankenhaft*). The substantiality of that which meets him is enlarged, and the way is prepared for more profound meeting—but also for more profound alienation if the I begins to rejoice in its state of separation and in the power it gains over the Other through objectification.

GATHERING THE THEMES TOGETHER (§§ 29–30)

THE OPENING LINE OF THE TEXT is repeated at this point, heralding a general recapitulation of the themes thus far orchestrated to form the conclusion to the first "movement": "To man the world is twofold, in accordance with his twofold attitude."

The It-World

The world as developed by our desire and need for security is a world organized for predictable experience and consequent utility. Being exists round about us as entities and their interchanges, but developed experience views them as things and processes (*Vorgänge*). "Thing" suggests a reduction to the lowest level of entity in the universe, that with which we are capable of least mutuality, that which can least respond to our presence, that, consequently, which appears the most indifferent to man. "Process," or *Vorgang,* is a term used to describe chemical reac-

---

139. Notice the contrast here between visual and aural metaphors. Buber sees this as the fundamental difference between the Western and the Oriental man: Western man is visual, Oriental man is aural ("Der Geist des Orients und das Judentum," *Reden,* JSJ, pp. 46–65). See WM, BMM, p. 127, on the Greek origin of the visual approach.

tions and hence suggests a mere mechanical and thus external relatedness—again something far removed from the demands of the Other who views us and calls out to us. Things are seen as composed of their characteristics and events, as divisible into moments. The original unity of entities in mutual interchange is broken up into smaller units of experience or thought, suggesting again that the face-to-face encounter between one total entity and another is beginning to lose hold. Thus man's initial detachment from the world of interaction is secured as he sets up a coordinate system of space and time within which to locate all things and processes. Such knowledge can be tucked away in the mind, mastered for further use.

To become aware of this ordered world is to enter into a community of truth where one can be understood with relative ease by others. But just as such an ordered world is not the ordering of the world, so such readily communicable truth is not truth in itself but truth as humanly constructed.[140] Underlying the constructed world order is a fundamental value-nihilism: the threat of nothingness stands over the I who dwells exclusively in the world of It—even though he may learn to dwell there collectively.

Thou

Authentic truth and value emerge when one moves out of this self-articulated ordering to meet what confronts him, not as an instance of this or that structure or as an object of this or that desire, but simply as an entity, in its wholeness and uniqueness. Primordial truth lies not in reflection but in commitment.[141] It is in this meeting, this commitment, that the self is enlarged, opening out to a sense of the totality available only through meeting. The light of the Thou bathes all things. The position seems not far removed from that of Heidegger.

The distinction between inner and outer (subject and object) loses its validity at this level, for meeting occurs in the depth which is the Between. Speaking subject-object language, we would have to say that the self exists *in itself* insofar as it exists *outside itself*, i.e., with the Other. And this is the depth,

140. See Anzenbacher, *Die Philosophie*, p. 58.
141. Emmanuel Levinas, "Martin Buber and the Theory of Knowledge," PMB, p. 141.

the "interior life," of the soul. The Thou informs the soul as the soul informs the body, each from its own distinct dimension which is not subject to the dimensions of bodily perceptions. The dimension of depth is the dimension of self-ecstatic mutuality where the self does not disappear in absorption but grows to its own selfhood and authentic differentiation.[142] It is in the depths of the Between, grounded upon spirit, that the opening to the Eternal Thou occurs. With the happy coming and the sad but inevitable going of the moments of relation with particular Thou's, there dawns the Thou Who can never become It (§ 61), Who is the consummation of relation as no particular Thou can be (§ 44).

Conclusion (§ 30)

One cannot live wholly with the Thou. As nature man has his needs, and as spirit he has his task, and out of these needs and this task the development of the world of It as man's becoming goes on and must go on. But one can come to live wholly in the world of It, urged on by the desire to remove the threat to the comfort and order of the It-world that comes with the unpredictable appearances of the Thou.[143] The Thou is simply not prepared for and is positively disallowed. The result is that technical progress can go on serving our needs, but inspiration disappears, for the wellsprings of the spirit have dried up. One who lives only with the It gradually falls away from being truly man. He oscillates from an individualism alienated from others to a collectivism of mutually alienated individuals bound together solely by needs.[144] Only if he returns to meeting and thus to authentic community will he return to himself.

142. Cf. the Hasidic notion of the sparks which belong to *one's own* soul ("Redemption," OMH, p. 207; "The Baal-Shem-Tov's Instruction," HMM, p. 189).
143. "Dialogue," BMM, p. 10.
144. WM, BMM, pp. 200 ff.

4 / Part Two: History and the Self

GROWTH OF THE IT-WORLD IN HISTORY (§§ 31–36)

PART ONE ENDED WITH THE ASSERTION that the world of It is essential to man, but one who lives exclusively within this world is not a man. This leads to the further elaboration of the It-world and to the further problems it raises for man. To these considerations Buber turns in Part Two.

The history of the individual and the race shows a progressive augmentation of the world of It. Cultures enlarge that world through their own experience and through the assimilation of the experience of other cultures preceding or contemporary with their own. Advancement of technical achievements, differentiation of social forms, and the expansion of speculative knowledge all add to the world of It. As this occurs, direct experience is replaced by indirect experience propagated in books and in the schools. And for the purpose of orientation and utility, indirect knowledge is sufficient. The individuals who are born into such situations are gradually weaned away from the immediacy of meeting and are taught to dwell in this world of indirection. Buber's description of the situation closely parallels that of Marcel.

Thinkers like Hegel often refer to this development in "objective mind" as progress in the "spiritual life." But because it drives man away from the Between, which is the locus of spirit, the development and use of the It-world actually becomes an obstacle to the real *life* of the spirit. Man's power to enter into relation

[73]

actually decreases with progress in objective knowledge and control (§ 31).

Having stated this position, Buber moves into the investigation of this inversely proportional development in the three regions of relation: with the forms of the spirit (§ 32), with one's fellow men (§§ 33–35), and with nature (§ 36).

Relation with the Forms (§ 32)

As we have already indicated (p. 36 f.), spirit itself is the word (*Wort*), the Between binding man to the Other and opening out as a relation to Transcendence. In the original relational event, in both the primitive and the child, spirit is there as ground of the relation. But spirit is *manifest* to man and in man only when man is capable of creative response (*Antwort*) to his Thou.[1] Now, response occurs in the three forms of the spirit: in knowledge, which terminates in *idea structures* as they find expression in language; in *art*, which terminates in the work; and in *pure action*, which terminates in a life formed in the spirit. In all three cases, the object structures which follow from the response are there for the community of other men who are to be drawn by these forms—in the same way that their creators were originally drawn—to a meeting in and through the world with that which transcends the world.[2] The highest of these forms is the third, because it is really that for the sake of which the other two regions of form exist: to form a life built upon constant openness to that which transcends the world as it manifests its Presence in and through the world.[3] The life that has become whole through constant meeting is the authentic *Tao*, the genuine teaching (*Lehre*), which has found its deepest expression

---

1. Walter Goldstein misses the important distinction between spirit *in itself*, as the Word which timelessly envelops nature, and spirit *in its human manifestation*, which arises through man's response to the Thou. Hence he will claim that spirit itself is the result of man. The opposite is the case for Buber (*Die Botschaft Martin Bubers*, Vol. II, *Der Dialogik universales Teil* [Jerusalem: Dr. Peter Freund, 1953], p. 67).

2. See "Postscript," *I and Thou*, p. 129.

3. See *Daniel*, p. 68; *Good and Evil*, trans. Ronald G. Smith (New York: Scribner's, 1953), p. 129; "Symbolic and Sacramental Existence," OMH, p. 163.

thus far in the Eastern world.[4] Here the Is and the Ought that have been fixed in Western science and law are transcended in a life open to the unpredictable flashes of Transcendence.[5]

The stronger the response made by the creative individual, the more impressive the objective embodiment which emerges. But the more impressive the embodiment, the more it is apt to become a mere item of interest within the humanly immanent world of It. The knowledge object becomes another objective item to master speculatively or to turn into pragmatic advantage; the art object becomes something for the critics to assess according to their canons; the formed life becomes another biographical item within the chronicles of the objective historian. In any case, that which in the object—the hidden Thou—originally spoke of Transcendence now joins the circle of immanence. A separate region of "spiritual life" emerges where spirit poses no demand but merely becomes a means for man's enjoyment and use (§ 33). But for Buber, real spiritual life has passed out of the forms at this point, for "all real living is meeting" (§ 14).

Relation with Men (§§ 33–35)

Modern culture is a human world filled with objects. Those brought up within it are those educated to enjoy and utilize the world as object and thus to dwell in actual separation from reality. Direct meeting of man with man becomes mediated by the kind of institutions that develop over the course of time and that gradually take on an independent status. Uprooted from the original relational events that gave birth to them, institutions gradually become more and more oppressive for the individual. But the individual himself has become no less uprooted; living in separation, he has nowhere to go in his retreat from the oppressive It-world except within himself, where he finds nothing but feelings. Marx and Freud between them have divided the field of modern human existence, with Marx analyzing the objective life of institutions and Freud the subjective life of feelings.[6]

Floundering about in the nihilistic world of empty subjects

4. "The Teaching of the Tao," PW, pp. 31–58, esp. pp. 34–38 and 45–50.
5. *Ibid.*, p. 32; see also "Spirit and Body," OMH, p. 127.
6. "The Gods of the Nations and God," IW, p. 211.

and oppressive objects, men have tried to overcome their alienation through a flight into the realm of collective feelings, such as
colored the *Jugendbewegung* at the turn of the century.[7] But
feelings always fail because they can reveal the Other only as
object-of-feeling, never as Thou. And "he who existentially
knows no Thou will never succeed in knowing a We." [8] Community cannot be founded upon feelings. Authentic community for
Buber is built upon the acceptance of otherness, upon a living
relation with our fellow men with a common reference to a
living center. This notion of a living center sounds like relation
to God,[9] but Buber relates it to the *zaddik,* or holy man, of the
Hasidic community.[10] The genuine *zaddik* is a man whose life
has been informed by the spirit, a man in whom the Transcendent shines through. It was about this sort of man that the
Hasidic settlements developed in a series of concentric circles
formed by the inner circle of close disciples, the stable surround-
ing community, and the periphery of travelers who came to seek
guidance from time to time.[11] Isolated Thou-relations may occur;
but if these are to be located within a community, the spiritual
leader is needed. When single Thou-relations and the presence
of a spiritual leader occur, men can authentically say "We." [12]

The establishment of this sort of community is based on
what Buber calls the "social principle," which is the most basic
principle of human togetherness, integrating the people "horizontally" in terms of relation to a center of meaning rooted in
the depth dimension. It has as its correlate the "political principle," which "vertically" integrates the people through a hierarchy
of functions in terms of objective tasks to be done.[13] When the

7. "Dialogue," BMM, p. 32.
8. "What Is Common to All," KM, p. 108.
9. This is especially so when Smith capitalizes "Center" in his
translation (p. 45). Pfuetze (*Self,* p. 266) follows him in this. Kohn
(*Martin Buber,* pp. 186–87) relates it to a leader.
10. IMB, p. 68; see also *Paths in Utopia,* trans. R. F. C. Hull
(Boston: Beacon Press, 1960), p. 135.
11. "Spirit and Body," OMH, pp. 130–31, 141–49. Since the *zaddik,* however, is the man formed in relation to God, ultimately those
who identify the center here with God are not really so far off the
mark.
12. "What Is Common to All," KM, pp. 108–9; WM, BMM, pp.
175–76.
13. "Society and the State," PW, pp. 161 ff.; "The Validity and
Limitation of the Political Principle," PW, p. 213.

political principle dominates and the social principle declines, we have the massive and chaotic swinging of the pendulum from individualism to collectivism,[14] from one extreme of inauthentic humanity to another; for they are opposites within the dimension of the subject-object dichotomy. Authentic humanity takes place in the Between.

Beneath the political and social structures there is a third region, which is the domain of the "economic principle." [15] The social principle is based on the will to enter into relation, the political principle on the will to power, and the economic principle on the will to profit. Modern public life has seen the gigantizing and centralizing of economic and political developments. There is nothing essentially wrong with this state of affairs, provided it is balanced off by a structurally rich society interposed between the centralized economic and political structures.[16] But what has characterized the modern world is precisely the pulverization of community and the domination of the political and economic principles,[17] so that a huge and complex shell emerges with no spiritual substance. The externalized individuals are herded together and treated as means to be utilized in the achievement of productivity and power.[18] Against this tendency the isolated individual with his "inner" life of feelings seeks to revolt, but with decreasing success.

The decisive point is not whether the state rules the economy, nor is it even whether freedom and equality are achieved —though these are surely important considerations. The choice is not between the apparent freedom of the United States and the apparent equality of the USSR.[19] Both are pseudo-forms, for genuine freedom and equality are possible only through genuine fraternity, where men stand in openness to the Other.[20] Where this occurs, work within the huge political and economic systems can take on meaning and joy, possession can evoke reverence and the spirit of sacrifice. Where it fails, man is divided from

14. WM, BMM, pp. 200–205.
15. *Paths in Utopia*, p. 96.
16. *Ibid.*, p. 80.
17. "Society and the State," PW, pp. 166–68.
18. "Productivity and Existence," PW, pp. 5–10.
19. Weltsch ("Nachwort," in Kohn, *Martin Buber*, p. 456) reports Buber's statement to this effect at a conference on the situation of the Jew in the USSR held at Paris, September, 1960.
20. "Hope for This Hour," PW, pp. 220–21.

man and the separate realm of "spirituality" flounders hopelessly and ineffectually in its vain efforts to inject life into the dead mechanism.

Life with Nature (§ 36)

Out of many meetings with nature over the course of generations, a culture comes to form its own peculiar view of nature, its *cosmos*. Its world conception is that which establishes a culture's mode of dwelling within the real world totality. And as a mode of dwelling, it is more a set of world images than a set of world concepts.[21] Within that cosmos, space and time are qualitatively differentiated. Space has its holy places where the gods dwell, and it has its places for men. Time is filled with holy feasts and song. These qualitative nuances stem from the center of meaning, which is encounter with the Transcendent.

But implicit in the situation is the mere quantitative differentiation of space and time, where each point in space and each instant in time are qualitatively equivalent: a smooth world within which the laws of causal necessity operate. Nature, viewed in terms of the subject-object relation, eventually appears as a massive unbroken web of necessary connections which dominate the whole of experience, both physical and psychological. "Causality has an unlimited reign in the World of *It*." It is a scientific world, necessary for man's orientation.

When meeting with the Thou begins to fade from the picture, the causal network comes to the fore and imposes a kind of domination. Loving destiny (*Schicksal*) becomes oppressive fate (*Verhängnis*). The transition can be traced in the history of civilizations: in the Indian world, *Karma* changes from loving dispensation, whereby life comes back again with the hope of higher forms of existence, into an oppressive tyranny, the weight of past life upon the present. In the Greek world there is the transition from the Parmenidean world of *Dikē*, which is the

21. "China and Us," PW, p. 123. Indeed, when one can no longer create a world image, there can be no human dwelling in the universe (WM, BMM, p. 133). This is precisely what has created one of the most serious problems for modern man: his profound homelessness, rooted in taking seriously the notion of infinity—for which there can be no image. But it is likewise this homelessness that has made this age most profoundly able to probe the question of man (*ibid.*, p. 126).

heavenly way along which universal fitness [22] rules. The stars and the cycle of births become more oppressive in the Stoic world, until, with Plotinus, one learns to escape the cycles through contemplative withdrawal and ecstatic fulfillment with the Alone, or, with Christ, one is redeemed from the control of alien powers to enjoy the freedom of the children of God.

The modern world has its own version of fate: the dogma of universal causality. Buber rejects the Spenglerian thesis that every culture is a self-contained organism with a predetermined life cycle, but he does affirm that through all cultures there has developed the gradual descent from the richness of primitive relation to a situation of mediation by complex It-structures: a situation entirely governed by law—the vital law of universal struggle, the psychological law which builds up the self from instincts, the social law by which development goes on in spite of human endeavor, and the cultural law of growth and decline. The cosmos has swallowed up man.

However, what makes all this appear to be fate, the grinding-out of a cosmic machinery in indifference to man, is simply man's *belief* in the dogma of universal causal necessity. With Bergson, again, Buber holds that necessity is simply the view which results from looking back over what has already transpired. What such a view misses is the free creative act as it develops in the present. Prior to the free act, any number of possibilities lie open; once the choice is made, an observer can see which of the possibilities were achieved and which of the motivations prevailed. Hence there appears an unbroken chain of causes and effects that stretches back endlessly in time: the world of It.

THE I AND THE IT-WORLD (§§ 36–43)

Transcendence of the It-World (§§ 36–37)

THE HEALTHY MAN is one who is able to rise above the oppression of the It-World without renouncing "the world."

22. *Geschick.* Smith translates it as "fate" (Smith, p. 55), which is its first meaning. But the context and its etymological relation with *Schicksal*, which is one of the terms Buber is using here for benign destiny, in direct contrast with *Verhängnis*, as oppressive fate, make it clear that the second meaning of *Geschick*—destiny as *fitness*, appropriateness—is what is here intended.

He knows a type of "causality" that is more than necessary sequence because he knows freedom in the mutual exchange (*Wechselwirkung*) between I and Thou. But it is not an aimless freedom based on the arbitrary choice of one among multiple possibilities within the logical net of the It-world. Such "freedom" is actually subservience to the domination of instinct or habit. Authentic freedom has its counterpart in destiny (*Schicksal*, from *schicken*, "to send"), in vocation (*Bestimmung*, from *stimmen*, "to call"). It is thus a freedom based on attentiveness to the summons which comes out of the present (§ 37). And what comes out is the union of that which wells up out of one's own depths with what meets one in the present,[23] of passion with direction,[24] of power with meaning.[25]

Power and passion are identified in the Hasidic tradition with the "evil urge," which must be redeemed by channeling it through direction, which furnishes meaning. This "evil urge" is that which threatens to take possession of us from below; but it is also that without which there is no true human life. It contains, like all creatures, a "holy spark" that must be released. It is the fundamental dynamic of life.[26] As with Scheler's *Geist* and *Drang*, it is in the welding of spirit (which is the Between) with instinct (which arises from below) that the great works of the spirit have their origin.[27]

However, the very decision reached in meeting forces man out to become creative in the world of It. He leaves the holy place of meeting in order to transform through fresh forms the place that has become unholy through the dominance of objectification, mediation, It. This rhythm of coming and going from meeting to the world of It "is inwardly bound up for him with the meaning and character of this life." Through turning back to meeting, new meaning is born upon the earth. Here Buber is again translating a Jewish conception into a universal notion: turning (*Umkehr, teshuva*) "stands at the center of the Jewish

23. See *Daniel*, pp. 49–59, for a poetic description of this phenomenon.
24. *Good and Evil*, p. 97.
25. *Daniel*, p. 53.
26. See "The Way of Man, According to the Teaching of Hasidism," HMM, p. 142; "The Beginnings," OMH, pp. 54–55, 78 ff.
27. WM, BMM, p. 190.

conception of the way of man." [28] It likewise stands at the center of *I and Thou*, for, with the announcement of the theme of turning, attention shifts to the individual who awakens to the emptiness and despair involved in the separate It-world and thus stands at the beginning of redemption (§ 37).

Individual and Person (§§ 37–41)

Buber attempts here to make specific the contrast he had set up aphoristically in the beginning of the work: "The I of the I-Thou relation is another I than the I of the I-It relation" (§ 1). The former he terms *Person,* the latter *Eigenwesen* [29] or *Individual.* The *Eigenwesen* lives for himself, and he lives in terms of the humanly woven network of things outside and the domination of his instincts and consequent feelings inside. He constantly interposes his subjective designs between himself and reality and thus becomes incapable of listening and responding to whatever might meet him out of the situation. The world merely mirrors back to him his own desires. He takes his stand in his bodily difference from all others and defines all things in relation to himself.

The *Eigenwesen* has two chief forms, as Buber points out elsewhere: [30] the *selfish man,* whose biological self-relatedness becomes pathological, and the *egotist,* who is a reflective type turned in upon himself. These correspond to two of the types mentioned in § 40: the wild, thoughtless individual and the glib, self-assured individual. A third type mentioned in § 40 is the one who recognizes his inner emptiness but tries to hide it from himself.

A *person,* on the contrary, is one whose whole being is an open sharing in that which transcends himself. [31] Person is de-

28. "The Way of Man," HMM, p. 164; "Redemption," OMH, p. 210; "The Faith of Judaism," IW, pp. 19–21.

29. *Eigenwesen* means literally "its-own-being," suggesting a holding onto oneself and thus an inability to share oneself with the Thou. This corresponds to the Hasidic distinction between the trivial ego and the deeper self ("The Way of Man," HMM, p. 159).

30. IMB, p. 116.

31. *Person* (with modifications) corresponds to Kierkegaard's *Einzelne, Eigenwesen* to Stirner's *Einzige* ("The Question to the Single One," BMM, p. 41; W I, p. 218). The latter terms in each set Wheelwright translates well as "focussed singularity" and "the soli-

fined in terms of that to which he responds: reality. Buber presents here the central ontological notion of his philosophy: "All reality is an activity in which I share without being able to appropriate for myself. Where there is no sharing, there is no reality" (§ 39).[32] Sharing without appropriation is what constitutes the Between: neither the self nor the Other is appropriated, but each comes to itself in the act of relation. The person is also the free man, one who "believes in reality, i.e., the real solidarity of the real duality, I and Thou." [33] Sharing in otherness without appropriation is, as in Heidegger, letting the Other be, in and for itself—not in indifference but rather in relation with that Other, so that otherness not only is but is likewise manifest. To the extent that otherness is manifest, to that extent the self becomes a sharer in reality.

Otherness is not fully manifest, however, until the separated I and the world of It have emerged. The Thou-saying of the child and the primitive is still immature because their I-saying is still immature. The accentuation of the distance between the self and the Other makes the possibility of identification more profound, for I-Thou is increasingly capable of being seen in its difference from I-It. Provided one is aware that one's reality is not found within oneself, since the essential twofoldness is lacking,[34] provided one sees one's distinctness not as the place from which to organize and utilize the Other but as the necessary framework through which Being can appear,[35] the reflective de-

---

tary one," respectively ("Buber's Philosophical Anthropology," PMB, pp. 75–76). The former is realized in participation, the latter in separation from the Other. (In Kierkegaard's view, the only Other to whom man should fully direct himself is God.)

32. Smith, p. 63. Note that "appropriation" here is *eignen*.

33. "Wirklichkeit; das heisst . . . die reale Verbundenheit der realen Zweiheit Ich und Du" (§ 37, W I, p. 118). The translation is my own; Smith's (p. 59) is simply wrong: "the real twofold entity *I and Thou*." There is not *one* entity—not even a twofold entity; rather there are two *distinct* entities, facing each other in their otherness but bound together by that very fact.

34. WM, BMM, pp. 179–80.

35. *Fassung des Seins* (W I, p. 121). Smith's "conception of Being" (Smith, p. 64) is hardly illuminating. Cf. Heidegger's *Da-sein* as the locus of Being, the place through which Being appears in the midst of beings, in "The Way Back into the Ground of Metaphysics," *Existentialism from Dostoevsky to Sartre*, ed. Walter Kaufmann (Cleveland: Meridian, 1956), pp. 212–13.

velopment of one's own self becomes preparation for mature encounter.

There is a kind of twin dialectical process operative here. One begins in an undifferentiated presence where the self and the Other are englobed with only a prereflective (grounding) differentiation. Through reflection one is enabled to uncover one's own subjectivity and thus develop the subjective grounds for "seeing the other side." Through a return to relation one is deepened, and thus the basis is developed for a more profound reflective self-discovery—and so on, in increasing depth. But cutting across this dialectical spiral is the dialectic between It and Thou, between objectification of the Other and presence to him. Presence evokes response in the form of the creation of objective structures which are welded into other objective structures gained from previous experience. Armed with this, one is enabled to move back into meeting with a more profound sense of the Thou—and so on, in another dialectical in-depth spiral. Through the coming and going of these twin dialectical processes the dimension of the Between, of presence, of depth, grows, and, with it, the person who shares in it. But there is another dialectical eddy within the self-other spiral, for within the self-relation there are two processes: objectification of self-structures and that self-presence involved in knowing oneself simply as being: "I am!" The Thou-It spiral likewise has its own side-eddy in the coming and going between the particularity of sense impressions and the universality of conceptual structures on the side of the It. In the healthy situation, all these dialectical swirlings feed into the central channel of reality which is the Between—the place of meeting; and the person matures. In the pathological situation, one or the other backward-bending process breaks off and develops on its own. The self moves along with the separation and becomes progressively more emptied of reality.

Buber admits that person and *Eigenwesen* are really abstract idealizations of two tendencies within each man. But there are some who live closest to the *Eigenwesen* pole and others who live closest to the person pole. Instances of the latter appear in history in the persons of Goethe, who embodied relation to nature, Socrates, who lived a life of interpersonal dialogue over-arched by listening to what comes from beyond, and Jesus, who realized in an overpowering way his relation to the Father

(§ 40). What is especially interesting about this combination is that all three men are creators of the forms of the spirit: Goethe is a creator of art forms, Socrates of idea structures, Jesus of religion. So we have the *Kunst* and *Erkenntnis* and *reine Wirken* of § 32, but as embodied in, and flowing from, relation with nature, with men, and with God. Buber has said elsewhere [36] that art fulfills our relation to nature, so that the correlation between Goethe, art, and nature is not simply coincidence. He has said further (§ 32) that the point of ideas is to become effective among men and that the fulfillment of life between men is love,[37] which is a kind of knowledge: [38] hence the correlation of Socrates, men, and knowledge. All these manifestations of spirit point to that which transcends the world; and the movement of transcending finds its culmination in religious manifestation.[39] And since not only Jesus, but also Goethe and Socrates, represents a life formed by the spirit, each is an example of *reine Wirken*— although Jesus is the purest example.[40] In all three men the saying of "I" manifests the pure form of person with scarcely a shadow of the *Eigenwesen.*

An inquirer makes his presence felt at this point (§ 41) by introducing, in an aside, one exception to the neat logic that has developed here in Buber's solitary reflection. There is, besides the *Eigenwesen,* contained within himself, and the person who more fully participates in reality, a third type, who knows no Thou but who is likewise not merely circling about himself; this one is so wholly taken up with the Cause dictated by the situation of his age that he sees himself and others merely as functions of that Cause. Such a man, in Buber's estimation, was Napoleon.

Awareness of Self-Contradiction (§§ 42–43)

Man has an a priori relation to the Other, inborn in the very structure of his nature. His being is being-toward, being out-

36. WM, BMM, p. 180.
37. *Ibid.*
38. "Dialogue," BMM, p. 29.
39. WM, BMM, p. 180.
40. See *Two Types of Faith,* trans. Norman Goldhawk (New York: Harper Torchbooks, 1961), p. 12 and *passim* for Buber's attitude toward Jesus: "From my youth onwards I have found in Jesus my great brother."

there with the Other. But precisely because this relation is founded upon openness to Transcendence, man is free to choose his relation or nonrelation to the entities he encounters. The historical situation in which we find ourselves is one in which a massive It-world promotes experience and use and consequently separate individuality. Man gets turned back into himself and falls away from reality. But insofar as his free movement is at odds with the flow of his nature, an inner contradiction emerges, an optical illusion [41] in which the self appears as the one encountered. He may attempt to cultivate this inward turning deliberately and call it "religion," but he will only find himself losing himself more deeply in the inward maze. (Buber here, as elsewhere, is evidently speaking out of his own experience.) Here he is at the edge of life.

Spurred on by the self-contradiction produced by his alienation from reality, he attempts to think his way through to life.[42] Inner experiences and techniques are of no avail. Thought fabricates for him two speculative world pictures, one of the universe, the other of the soul. The world picture of the universe swallows up the self in its immensity and necessity; the world picture of the soul dissolves the universe into states of mind. In either case there is a reduction in which one of the partners obliterates the other: *Hen panta*, One becomes All. (Buber elsewhere terms one of these reductions *cosmologism*, the other *psychologism*.) [43] Armed with these speculative constructions, when the unknown abyss of the self or of the world opens up to man and fills him with horror, he can quell that horror either through deceiving himself that there is no self or through imagining that the self is the All, so that in either case nothing can happen to the self. But the time comes when both pictures are seen together. The secu-

---

41. *Doppelgängertum* (§ 42, W I, p. 126). Smith (p. 70) merely transliterates it as "doubleganger." In everyday German usage the term refers to "look-alikes," people who may be confused with each other because of their resemblance. As a technical term in psychology it refers to a special kind of optical illusion where a shift in attention yields a different *Gestalt* with the same data.

42. This last section (§ 43) of Part Two is clearly autobiographical. "That which lies there with cruel eyes," once his playfellow, recalls Buber's description of his cat; his alienation now recalls his description of an experience with his horse ("Dialogue," BMM, p. 23).

43. "Von der Verseelung der Welt," *Nachlese*, p. 149.

rity furnished by cosmologism and psychologism is seen as resting upon an abstraction. "And a deeper shudder seizes him."

Buber cuts off Part Two at this point and leaves the reader hanging as to the reason for that deeper shudder. And perhaps part of the reason for the puzzlement is that the reader expects to move from pseudosecurity to real security, whereas for Buber all security is illusory, whether it be the security of speculative construction, ethical norms, or objects of belief or the securities of routine existence.[44]

Between psychologism and cosmologism lies *ontologism*,[45] which locates the problem of human existence in the Between. But it gives no final answers. The Between has no smooth continuity, but from time to time it breaks through the world of It for one who is attuned.[46] This is the "narrow ridge" provided by the situation, the realm of radical responsibility. As Buber sees it, this is no relativism but an indistinguishable admixture of conditionality and unconditionality: the conditionality of the historical, social, and psychological situation and the unconditionality of our openness to what reveals itself in the situation.[47]

44. "Dialogue," BMM, pp. 16–18; §§ 59, 61.
45. "Von der Verseelung," *Nachlese,* p. 149.
46. "The Baal-Shem-Tov's Instruction," HMM, p. 184.
47. "Zur Situation der Philosophie," *Nachlese,* pp. 136–38.

5 / Part Three: The Eternal Thou

WE NOW REACH, in Part Three, the point of Buber's "most essential concern," namely, "the close connection of the relation to God with relation to one's fellow-man." [1] This part unfolds as follows. The first four sections (§§ 44–48) deal with the relation between meeting God and meeting the finite Thou. Buber then moves into an extended critique of other positions which tend to minimize one or the other of the partners in relation (§§ 49–51). Various aspects of the way in which the *world* of relation is built up in relation to God are then treated (§§ 52–60). The conclusion of the work focuses upon the way God's revelation enters into and affects the development of human history (§ 61).

GOD AND THE FINITE THOU (§§ 44–48)

IF ONE FOLLOWS OUT the basic *élan* involved in relations to the finite Thou, one discovers, Buber claims, that they all point beyond themselves to the Thou Who can never become an It. Buber comments in a later work: "That the lines of these relations intersect in the eternal Thou is grounded in the fact that the man who says Thou ultimately means his eternal Thou." [2] How is this so? Because in every relation "the primary Word addresses the eternal Thou" (§ 44). In relation, man *steps into* the primary Word (§ 3), i.e., into the Between, the region of spirit which is a reference to the Transcendent. The knowing of

1. "Postscript," *I and Thou*, pp. 123–24; IMB, p. 99.
2. IMB, p. 114.

otherness is grounded upon this transcendent reference (see p. 64, above); and that reference, in turn, is realized only *through* relation to the finite Thou. Similar to Kantian doctrine, this a priori structure is brought to light only by reference to a "material" content. The "content" here is the finite Thou. That does not make the finite Thou into a mere means,[3] since it is only in full response to the uniqueness of the individual in and for itself that the relationship with God is established. The individual must be taken seriously for itself before it furnishes an opening to the Transcendent. In a sense there is a mutual mediation here, for only when one meets the finite Other unconditionally—and thus with reference to the Unconditioned—does the finite Thou manifest itself; and only where the finite Thou manifests itself is the presence of the eternal accessible.[4]

Every finite Thou as a Thou speaks of the eternal Thou. But this is manifest only reflectively, because every finite Thou is fated to become an It (§ 22), thereby drawing our attention out beyond all finitude to the eternal Thou Who can never become an It (§ 48).[5] The a priori orientation of the self is actualized in each relation to a finite Thou, but fulfillment is possible only in relation to the eternal Thou (§ 44).

The language one may come to use in addressing the eternal Thou is a secondary matter. With the primitives, words of presence were used; with the moderns, more abstract terms are employed. But the latter often stand in the way of really saying *Thou*, so that some are forced to reject the God named by abstractions and thus become "atheists." What really matters is

3. As John Cullberg asserts (*Das Du und die Wirklichkeit* [Uppsala Universitets Årsskrift; Uppsala: Lundeqvistska, 1933], pp. 44–45). Smith misleads the English readers by translating "*durch* jedes geeinzelte Du" (italics mine) as "by means of every particular Thou," whereas "*through*" more properly carries the meaning intended. Buber knew—even better than Kant—that a person, and indeed every creature, is an end, not a means.

4. This analysis gets us out of the knots within which Nathan Rotenstreich is entangled over this relation ("Some Problems," pp. 156–59).

5. Arno Anzenbacher calls this position on God, as the Thou Who can never become It, the basic thesis of dialogical thinking as philosophy of religion ("Thomismus und Ich-Du Philosophie," *Freiburger Zeitschrift für Philosophie und Theologie*, XII, No. 2–3 [1965], 185–86).

that one really says *Thou* in an unconditional way—even if such a one happens to be an "atheist." At one level the problem of atheism and theism is a function of the conditioned character of the conceptual and emotional equipment of the age; but at the fundamental level it is a matter of meeting or its absence (§ 45).

At this point (§ 46) Buber examines once more the meeting of will and grace described earlier (§ 14). But here he focuses attention upon the will side of the relation, for the part we know is only our side of the meeting. Even that part Buber describes only negatively: there is no going beyond sense experience, no recourse to a separate realm of ideas, no prescriptions for special spiritual exercises, no giving-up of the I. Only by doing it can one really learn what it means to enter into relation. In entering into relation there occurs the indivision of the self, the "becoming whole" which again is negatively described as the suspension of all partial activities.

Notice that the description of becoming whole begins from the situation of the dividedness of the separated I. Notice that the same is true with regard to our access to what meets us from the other side: the Thou appears as totalized, i.e., again, undivided. Philosophy, which is the supreme achievement of the subject-object dichotomy, setting off things as clearly and distinctly as possible,[6] is here led beyond itself [7] to the point where the undivided meets the undivided. Buber begins with the subject-object relation, which involves, as he sees it, multiple acts of intending and multiple aspects intended. He then progressively negates, first, the multiple structure of the object, then the multiple structure of the self. Hence, as we have already indicated, his thinking has been termed a *negative* ontology.[8] This gives some specification to the function of the It-world in the maturing of man's relation to the Thou: it plays a negative role in teaching us more and more deeply the meaning of dividedness and separation from ultimate meaningfulness, and thus, by contrast, it can develop in us more profoundly the desire for and appreciation of unity (cf. § 61).

The phenomenon of becoming whole is frequently described

6. EG, p. 45.
7. IMB, p. 17.
8. Theunissen, "Bubers negative Ontologie," pp. 323–28.

by Buber as preparatory to meeting and thus as something apparently achievable prior to meeting (§§ 46, 50).[9] However, elsewhere he says unequivocally: "Man can become whole not in virtue of a relation to himself but only in virtue of a relation to another self."[10] This seems to preclude what he says in the other places cited. But if we notice, in both of these contexts (§§ 46, 50) he is speaking of preparation for the *supreme meeting*, i.e., the meeting with the eternal Thou. Hence the position is secured that only through meeting can one gain one's own unity: only one who meets the finite Thou has the self-unity requisite for meeting the eternal Thou. And it is such a one, likewise, who can truly perform the works of the spirit.[11]

There is, however, another text where Buber clearly speaks of achieving "the power of concentrated being" by turning aside (§ 48). The only way this can be seen as not contradicting his other assertion—that only through relation to another does one become whole—is by distinguishing the wholeness of *life* from the wholeness achieved in withdrawal. In the latter case Buber speaks of "the *soul's* becoming one." The soul can gather up its power in isolation; but the person can be established in his psychophysical unity only through meeting another.[12] It is clear that, for Buber, only the unity achieved in meeting is total unity (§ 48).[13]

Every meeting with an entity (*Wesen*) or a form (*Wesenheit*)[14] in the world stands out in an exclusiveness which reveals an absolute uniqueness, though it stands out against the complementary background of the others who are illumined by it. If the Other becomes an object, its exclusiveness becomes separateness and exclusion of the others. But "in the relation with God, unconditional exclusiveness and unconditional inclusiveness are one" (§ 47). The exclusiveness is unconditional because God is the Wholly Other; but the inclusiveness is likewise unconditional because God is nearer to things than they are to themselves.

If we grant that there is a God and a world, then there are

9. Smith, p. 89.
10. WM, BMM, p. 168.
11. See also "The Way of Man," HMM, pp. 148–51; § 50.
12. See "Man and His Image Work," KM, p. 151.
13. See also EG, p. 44.
14. Smith's "life" is simply wrong.

three speculative possibilities of understanding their relation: (1) God and world are separate, (2) God is in the world, and (3) the world is in God. In the first case, Buber claims, we are supposed to come to God by turning away from the world; but by turning from things, one only confronts nothing.[15] This does not mean that there is nothing apart from things. (Buber accepts God's transcendence of the world.) It means that man can approach God only through things, which are His medium of communication with man. In the second case, one supposedly finds God by remaining in the world; but by attempting to fathom the world, one only comes up with the insoluble.[16] In the third case, one goes out, but not away from, things, carrying them all with him to meet God. In keeping life holy, one encounters the living God as the One Who encompasses and speaks through all things. In freeing the appearances through the coming-together of our attitude and the grace of the Other, we allow God to dwell in the world.[17]

For Buber, God can be met in and through the world, but He cannot be sought or inferred. He cannot be sought because He is everywhere to be found. Turning aside from the world may bring the wisdom of solitude, which is the place where philosophy develops;[18] one may gain concentration of soul; but God does not appear in this way.[19] Every encounter with the finite Other gives man a glimpse of fulfillment. In composed expectation he meets and aids the Others, until in the ultimate meeting he can

15. See "The Question to the Single One," BMM, pp. 52, 58.

16. *Unauflösbare.* This presupposes Buber's acceptance of the Kantian theory of knowledge, which claims that any attempt at ultimate unification of knowledge runs into insoluble antinomies (*Critique of Pure Reason*, A 406–567, B 432–595).

17. See §§ 49–51. Hartshorne and Reese see in Buber all the elements of a panentheist position which conceives of God as eternal as well as temporal, conscious of Himself and aware of, as well as including (though not identical with), the world (Charles Hartshorne and William Reese, *Philosophers Speak of God* [Chicago: University of Chicago Press, 1953], pp. 16 ff. and 302–6; see also Hartshorne's "Martin Buber's Metaphysics," PMB, pp. 49–68).

18. WM, BMM, pp. 126, 199.

19. For Buber there is the call to meeting in worldless solitude (see § 61; IMB, p. 86), but the point he is making here is that this cannot be *sought*. Even in the case of a special call, one must remain attached to and return to speak in the community (see below, p. 96).

gather them all up (see p. 99, below). All encounter with the finite Other leads up to encounter with the eternal Thou. But this is not the end of the journey. Here man merely finds the eternal Center, out of which all meaning streams into the whole of the way.

If God cannot be sought, neither for Buber can He be inferred, whether in the subject, as the Self which thinks itself in the subject;[20] in nature, as its author; or in history, as its master. God can only be addressed. No reason is given; the position is merely stated. But it is a position which follows from the Kantian theory of knowledge, which Buber indeed accepts, and from a fideism which sees in proof a threat to faith.[21] He finds corroboration of the Kantian position in the insoluble antinomy between freedom and dependency in man (§ 51) and in the theory of complementarity in contemporary physics, which is simply the acceptance of the contradiction involved in the data.[22] For Buber the ultimate mysteries of creation are beyond logic and hence beyond proof.[23] Buber will likewise insist that even if one could develop a sequence of ideas which culminated in the notion of God, all one would end up with would be a *notion-God* and thus not God at all.[24] Hence Buber will cite with approval Pascal's distinction between the God of the philosophers and the living God of Abraham, Isaac, and Jacob.[25]

The essential thing is that one learn to address God as the perpetually nearest One Who stands over against us as the supreme Partner in dialogue. But, that dialogue may occur, it is essential that the independence of both partners be maintained.

CRITIQUE OF MYSTICISM (§§ 49–50)

THERE ARE TWO POSITIONS, however, which destroy the essential prerequisites for dialogue by the absorption of one

20. God cannot be inferred "aus dem Subjekt als das Selbst, das sich in ihm denkt" (§ 48). The reference is evidently to German Idealism, where God completes Himself through thinking Himself in human awareness (see WM, BMM, p. 139). Smith's "God cannot be inferred . . . in the subject as the self that is thought in it" is just not in the German text.

21. IMB, p. 84.

22. "Man and His Image Work," KM, p. 156.

23. WM, BMM, pp. 188–89; "Replies," PMB, pp. 690, 701.

24. EG, p. 54.

25. EG, pp. 49–50, 62.

partner or the other. Encounter with these positions is crucial, since Buber attempts to base his philosophy entirely upon experience, and there are two forms of experience which seem directly to contradict his fundamental position.[26] In one position (represented by Schleiermacher) the self pole is collapsed by reducing relation to God to a feeling of dependency (§ 49). This has its extreme form in a mystical position where God is seen either as drawing up the self into an identity with Him (*ecstasy*, the self's "standing-out" from itself) or as entering into and taking over the self (*enthusiasm*, the "indwelling of God"). Though such an experience begins in the duality of the partners—God and the self—it ends in their identity. The other position, which is found chiefly in the mystics of India, collapses the divine pole by reducing all to the self. Here the originally given duality of God and the self is surpassed by the insight into its illusory character. Both are positions which Buber himself had earlier accepted.

The first of these two positions begins most clearly in the person and sayings of Jesus—especially in his claim that "I and the Father are one"—and culminates in Eckhart's mystical doctrine of the birth of the Godhead in the soul. But the tradition really has no firm basis in Christ, as Buber sees it. Knowledge and love join Father and Son, but not on equal footing. The Father is recognized as the greater. From His side come mission and command; from the Son's, seeing and hearkening. Hence the "are one" in the above passage involves, not absorption, but relation in its purest form (cf. § 40). The mystical doctrine which draws upon such texts is experientially based upon real meeting with the Thou. But the I is carried on by "the dynamic of relation itself" into the illusory experience from which both I and Thou seem to disappear. Reality grows dim at this point.[27] Authentically considered, this dynamic is the spontaneous movement from the mutuality of the relational event to an inevitable separation of the partners which can culminate in a self-experience of authentic solitude, an experience of the self as it grows

26. Buber's recognition of the importance of this encounter is indicated by the length he gives to this treatment: fourteen pages, the most extensive treatment in the book. Because this encounter is central to understanding the whole development of Buber's thought, we have developed the textual background at some length in Chapter 1.

27. See "Dialogue," BMM, p. 18.

in and through relation.[28] Attempting deliberately to follow that movement can lead to a sense of fullness that appears to transcend both the self and the Other.

Buber declares this position illusory for two reasons: (1) it destroys his basic principle that reality lies only in meeting and thus in identity-in-difference; (2) it splits man's life into two: the "higher" moments of "illumination" and the "lower" moments of "fallenness" in the everyday world. The two principles are bound together in that the bulk of man's life has to do with the Other, and it is in relation to the Other that the total body-soul unity is achieved. The unity involved in separation (either pre- or postrelational) is only the unity of the *soul*. It cannot be the unity of *life*. Any attempt to make it so is bound to lead to unreality.[29]

The Indian position begins in the doctrine of the Upanishads that the real is the self, and it culminates in the person of the Buddha. According to Buber, it is clear that Buddha himself knows the *Thou*-saying to men and knows the "undivided confrontation of the undivided Mystery." [30] But Buddha ultimately rejects as illusory the world of sense forms in which the human Thou appears, and of relation to the eternal Thou he keeps silent. In the last analysis the Unborn is within the self; through ascetic withdrawal Buddha kills in himself the ability to say *Thou* and thereby claims release from the Wheel of Rebirth (§ 50).[31]

In identifying the self, the Upanishads appeal to the condition of deep, dreamless sleep—without desire, even without consciousness—where unity is experienced.[32] Though such a doctrine appears identical with becoming whole—in both its preparatory form preceding relation in the unification of the soul and its fuller form of life totality within relation—it is not the same. It is rather annihilation than unity, for it depends upon

28. "Von der Verseelung der Welt," *Nachlese*, p. 154: "Das, was zwischen mir an dieser Beziehungsfläche der Seele (zwischen mir und der Welt) in seiner Dynamik (*Zueinander, Auseinander, Einsamwerden*) aufsteigt und zu Bewusstsein wird, das ist Selbsterfahrung eines durch natürliches Wachstum des Bewusstseins Erworbenes." (Italics mine.)

29. "Foreword," PW, pp. xv–xvi.

30. See EG, pp. 27–28.

31. Smith, pp. 90–93.

32. See "What Is Common to All," KM, pp. 94–96.

the elimination of everything within and without the self. It attempts to move back into a pure subject of thinking, but without any object of thought. But a subject of thinking is precisely defined by its object; [33] and it is no wonder that such a subject, removed from its object, can appear as nothing (or as All, since there is no longer any basis for comparison with, and thus delimitation by, others).[34] One could also form a thought object which one might then call "the subject." However, this is, strictly speaking, inconceptualizable; it is merely posited as the ultimate ground of all objectification at the ideal limit of a reflective regress.[35] One could likewise conceive of such an objectless subject by anticipating the situation of death. These are interesting experiments, but for Buber they have nothing essential to do with *life*, which is found only in mutual interchange. Any attempt to base a life upon them is merely an exalted form of self-deception.[36] They must feed back into the totality of man's relations.

However, the Indian doctrine does have a contribution to make, insofar as it leads to the becoming-one of the soul (which is preparatory to its "annihilation"). But the becoming-one of the soul is only preliminary.[37] It is necessary for the work of the spirit, but it is not the same as the becoming-one of the whole body-soul person, which is possible only through meeting.[38] "The central reality of the everyday hour on earth, with a streak of sun on the maple twig and the glimpse of the eternal *Thou*, is greater for us than all enigmatic webs on the brink of being." [39] Mysticism proposes, as an ideal, a flight from the world which is given to us. But it is a flight into an enigmatic world at best, a flight from the full unity of the self and a flight from that world where we know the eternal Thou can be met. The only world

33. See EG, pp. 39–40.
34. "Dialogue," BMM, p. 25.
35. "Ein Denkendes für sich gibt es—im Denken, als dessen Erzeugnis und Gegenstand nämlich, als vorstellungsfreien Grenzbegriff" (W I, p. 138). The reference is evidently to the Kantian transcendental Ego. Smith's translation (p. 90) of the last two words reads: "as a limiting idea without an imaginable subject."
36. "Foreword," PW, p. xvi.
37. Smith, p. 92.
38. Smith, p. 89. See also "Man and His Image Work," KM, p. 151; "Brother Body," PW, pp. 20–24.
39. Smith, pp. 87–88.

where God cannot be met is the world of It, and that is because it is not the real world.

However, Buber does speak as though a genuine meeting with God can be achieved in solitude. In § 61, for example, he speaks of being summoned out of the community "into the final solitude" to meet with God. In a later work,[40] in response to an inquiry as to whether there is meeting with God apart from meeting with the creature, Buber replies that there are hours where one is "alone with the Alone," as testified to by a vast literature throughout the ages.[41] Again, he speaks of both the authentic mystical experience and the achievement of artistic vision as experiences in which the mystic and the artist cling to the common world of men until they are forcibly torn from it. Indeed, being drawn beyond the community and its *cosmos* is essential to all creative encounter with the forms of the spirit, for this is the only way in which new forms can be born into the human world. Thus the decisive matter is whether or not one remains attached and attuned to the community.[42] Hence Buber will say that "we expect a theophany of which we know nothing but the place, and the place is called community." [43] If there is a withdrawal from the community, it is only for the sake of a return, to enrich the community. Meeting with God involves mission to the world (cf. § 61). If relation to the world disappears, God disappears with it, and only the isolated soul remains.[44]

In § 49, where he is dealing with the feeling of dependency, Buber treats of a theme that he picks up again at the end of § 50 and once more in § 51: the antinomic character of our side of

40. IMB, p. 86.

41. The question was raised by Maurice Friedman, *the* expert on Buber in America. The fact that Friedman himself was puzzled about this relation indicates that Buber has not expressed himself clearly at all in this regard. Philip Wheelwright ("Buber's Philosophical Anthropology," PMB, p. 78) interprets Buber to mean that there is no relation to God apart from relation to one's fellow men. Buber says he "read this with some surprise" ("Replies," PMB, p. 710). Relation with God is possible in every situation, but "the essential relation to God must find its complement in the essential relation to men."

42. "What Is Common to All," KM, pp. 101–2.

43. "Dialogue," BMM, p. 7.

44. "Spinoza, Sabbatai Zvi, and the Baal-Shem," OMH, p. 95.

meeting with God as dependency and freedom in one and the same act. This is a situation in which, for Buber, the principle of contradiction does not hold.[45] Man needs God—for Buber that seems obvious; but he goes further—*God also needs man*. First, in order that the meaning of man's life *as man* be fulfilled, man's freedom must be included (otherwise the fulfilled life is not man's); thus God needs man for the meaning of man's life. But God also needs man for His own fate in the world (§ 49). Behind these notions again lies Hasidism, with its roots in the Old Testament. God as *Elohim*, as the Transcendent, is the creator Who pours His strength into His creatures; but God as YHWH involves His personal address to man. When man responds, God's glory is realized, His immanence is fulfilled, His Shekinah comes to rest in the world; or God loses, through man's failure to respond.[46] "The world is not divine sport, it is divine destiny" (§ 49).

Hence the teaching of divine immanence involves for Buber a *relation* between God and man in which *becoming* is introduced into God Himself. On this basis, Brown asks, "In the end, is Buber merely an existentialist veneer upon Hegel?"[47] There are many resemblances between Buber and Hegel, and yet the differences outweigh the samenesses. The "veneer" reaches to the heart of Buber's vision, for Buber overturns Hegel's notion of perfection through mediation in terms of the primacy of immediate presence. Furthermore, he sees man's relation to God as person to Person and not, as in Hegel, a relation of person to the Absolute Principle.[48]

45. "The Faith of Judaism," IW, p. 17.
46. "Spirit and Body," OMH, p. 117; "God and the Soul," OMH, pp. 194–99; "Hasidism and Modern Man," HMM, p. 35; "The Way of Man," HMM, p. 127.
47. James Brown, *Kierkegaard*, p. 126.
48. Brown (*ibid.*, pp. 117–18) and Agus (*Modern Philosophies*, p. 244) are misled into conceiving the whole situation as pantheistic by following Smith's translation: "God comprises, but is not, the universe. So, too, God comprises, but is not, my self" (Smith, p. 95). "Comprises" is one translation of *umfasst*, but the context—and even the very passage—makes it clear that *encompasses* is the intended meaning. Cullberg (*Das Du*, p. 45), following the German text, makes the same mistake. See "The Way of Man," HMM, pp. 126–27 on the rejection of pantheism along with a simultaneous acceptance of the divine immanence and transcendence.

As a matter of principle, Buber insists that he makes no statements as to the nature of God in Himself.[49] But as a matter of fact, he is here making two claims about God's nature: that God is related to man and thus is involved in becoming.[50] He will later use the language of Spinoza to speak of the attributes of God as natural and spiritual being, grounding the natural and spiritual being of creatures; and he will add as well that God as personal being is the ground of man's dialogical personality.[51] These claims seem clearly to involve a causal inference based on the assumed principle that effects do not exceed, and that they in some way mirror, their causes. And behind that assertion lies another claim: that God is the Creator. This follows from the experience of things as revealing God, the way words reveal the person of any speaker. Creation is the word of God to man.[52]

GOD AND THE WORLD (§§ 52–60)

Establishing the World of Relation (§§ 52–54)

THE MANIFESTATION of the creaturely Thou, whether it is an animal, a stone, or another human, is always fleeting: either the self or the Other is not fully there, not fully open.[53] This is not a fault; it is simply the creaturely condition. But even here there is the possibility of remaining as open as we can to

49. "Replies," PMB, p. 690.
50. Cf. Charles Hartshorne, "Martin Buber's Metaphysics," PMB, pp. 49–68. Hartshorne attempts to develop this into a metaphysics of relation and becoming, although Buber rejects the attempt as inadequate to his own position ("Replies," PMB, pp. 614–15). These two claims are in contrast to the Scholastic tradition, which is careful to insist that God is not related to creatures and that, in contrast to the realm of creatures who come to be, God simply *is* and is in no way involved in becoming.
51. "Postscript," *I and Thou*, pp. 134–37.
52. See below, p. 99. Brown (*Kierkegaard*, p. 117), in his accusation of pantheism, has to claim (wrongly) that Buber does not accept a Creator, and then goes on to add that, if he did, his position would be adequately grounded.
53. Though this is undoubtedly true of beings *qua* conscious, it seems to contradict that which he had said previously (see above, p. 49) about the presence of all beings simply as being there. In that case it is only the self who is absent, not the finite Other.

the manifestations of the Thou and thus of being related in an alternating rhythm of actual and potential relation.

In pure relation with the eternal Thou, however, it is only we who are absent; hence, Buber says, the eternal Thou by its nature can never become an It. Here we begin to see the extent to which Buber takes the notion of mutuality in the Thou-relation. *Thou* is not just a matter of our attitude. *Thou* is a perfection, not of our side of the relation alone, but of the Other as well. Just as the self can become itself only through the gift of the Other, so likewise the Other can become itself only through the gift of the self. Through our open response, when will and grace meet, the "sparks" are released from things and brought to fulfillment. However, in the case of God, He is always present, always fully there, perfected as Thou (§§ 52–53).[54]

Through many meetings with finite Thou's, it can come to pass that one begins to recognize a single Voice that speaks to us through the many occurrences.[55] Buber is here giving witness to his own life, where many relations with beings culminated in a single experience of faith;[56] it is this experience that brings into being the *world* of relation. The world is manifest as divine language (§ 56).[57] And this is, fundamentally, the reason why every finite Thou is a glimpse through to God.[58] Buber's position here calls to mind Bonaventure's assertion that the world is a book written by God and addressed to man. Just as we might concern ourselves with the structure of the book, the number of pages, the frequency of occurrence of certain words, the style of the print, and so forth, so we might become preoccupied with the

54. Here again, Brown's alignment of Buber with Hegel is refuted. However, the reconciliation of this position with the position of creation as divine destiny (§ 49) is not at all apparent—though Buber finds no problem with this, since the whole situation transcends the principle of contradiction!

55. "Dialogue," BMM, pp. 14–15.

56. "Replies," PMB, pp. 689–90. Notice that, if one does not accept the experiential character of Buber's assertions, one is forced to claim with Cullberg (*Das Du*, pp. 44–45) that God is *postulated* to develop continuity among man's many individual Thou-encounters.

57. See "My Way to Hasidism," HMM, p. 49: "In Hasidic teaching, the whole world is only a word out of the mouth of God." See also "Spinoza," OMH, p. 91.

58. See Anzenbacher, *Die Philosophie*, p. 66.

objectifiable structures of the world. But unless we go beyond that to what is being said, and ultimately to the One Who says it, our analysis is fruitless.[59]

This attention to the One Who speaks is man's fundamental act of turning to the Center from which meaning streams into man's world. But it is not merely the world-for-man that is affected. Buber here (§ 54) moves beyond the initial position from which the text developed: that the world *for man* is two-fold (§ 1). In virtue of the fact that man emerges from the cosmos itself, the twofold structure of estrangement from and turning to the Source, found in man in the I-It and I-Thou relations, is the fundamental structure of the universe itself. This universe is set on the course of *Becoming* which man carries on; but it is in man also that the very *Being* of the universe is produced through his development of the Between, which arises as such only through man.[60] It is again a fundamental Hasidic concept that Buber here takes up: ". . . man is commissioned and summoned as a cosmic mediator to awaken a holy reality in things through holy contact with them."[61] This echoes, from a Jewish point of view, the perennial wisdom of the East.[62] Here is Buber's fundamental position:

> . . . every investigation of a subject in its conditioning by the manner, the nature, the attitude of man leads us towards the subject's place in being and its function in meaning. For according as we fathom the relation of a circuit of reality to us, we are always referred to its still unfathomed relation to Being and meaning.[63]

Sprung from the cosmos, man is fundamental openness to the Transcendent, grounded in spirit. Through man's relation to the Thou in all finite things, he and the things with him are drawn into the Between, expressly related to Transcendence. They become Thou. That means: they enter into their own being. Man produces "the being of the world."[64]

---

59. *In Hexaemeron* XII, Peltier edition, Vol. IX, p. 88a.
60. "Distance and Relation," KM, p. 63.
61. "Hasidism and Modern Man," HMM, p. 33.
62. "Der Geist des Orients und das Judentum," *Reden,* JSJ, p. 51.
63. "Man and His Image Work," KM, pp. 149–50.
64. "Distance and Relation," KM, p. 63.

God and the Regions of Relation (§§ 55–60)

At this point Buber repeats the main themes of § 9. The three spheres in which the world of relation is built—our life with nature, with men, and with the forms of the spirit—are all pervaded by the Presence manifested in the Between, which, like Heidegger's Being, exists only through man. Through the forms of the spirit, the relation to the eternal Thou is spelled out in the It-world of human becoming. But it is possible for man, by very reason of the original distance given him by spirit, to remove the spheres of relation from presence. The mighty works of the spirit rigidify: knowledge creates a comfortable and smooth world of consistency that functions as a surrogate for real relation with nature; love develops into an interhuman world of fixed proprieties [65] behind which men can cloak their feelings and which they can substitute for real relation; creative activity settles down into a set of canons for correct procedure (*Gültigkeit*). It is a secure world that emerges in this way, but it is no longer theophany. Total meaningfulness has drained from it, and an impressive but empty shell remains. Man may attempt to give glitter to it by gracing these abstractions with the glorious names of Cosmos, Eros, and Logos. But the real Cosmos exists for man when he dwells in nearness to things, genuine Eros only in authentic community, and real Logos only in open response to the spirit developed anew in every age (§ 55).[66]

Of these three regions, the center is life with men. It is only through life with men that an authentic cosmos arises; [67] it is to men that the creative personalities speak in the works of the spirit they form. It is in the encounter with men, where response is open and in the form of language, that the primal experiential analogate of man's relation with God is formed (§ 56). Even though the Between is involved in every response to the Thou— in the regions of nature and the forms of the spirit as well as in the region of men—relation in the realm of the human community is the real bearer of the Between.

> Man has always thought his thoughts as I, and as I he has transplanted his ideas into the firmament of the spirit, but as We

65. *Affizierbarkeit*, literally "sensitivity."
66. "What Is Common to All," KM, pp. 104–5.
67. *Ibid.*, p. 91; WM, BMM, p. 155.

he has ever raised them into being itself, in just that mode of existence that I call "the between" or "betweenness." That is the mode of existence between persons communicating with one another.[68]

The way in which man stands in the presence of nature and the forms of the spirit, and ultimately in the Presence of God Himself, is rooted in the mode of being of the human community. The *Zwischen* itself is articulated through the *Zwischenmenschlichen*. All relation to nature and to the forms of the spirit is conditioned by the community and circles back into the community to contribute toward the becoming of human history.

"Is there a fourth possibility?" the ever present inquirer asks. Besides life with nature, with men, and with the forms of the spirit, is not solitude a way to the eternal Thou? For Buber, solitude and relation are the systole and diastole of the soul[69] and are not to be broken apart. To solitude one retires in order to become free of the world of It and to gather up the powers of the soul.[70] It is in solitude that the deepest questions arise.[71] But reality occurs only in the Between, and the answers lie only in meeting. Solitude is only a necessary preparation for more profound meeting. To remain in solitude is to sink into unreality and self-contradiction. Hence the real point of solitude is not to close but "to keep open the gates of finitude."[72]

The conversion that emerges out of self-gathering and questioning in solitude is not simply a matter of substituting a new object for man's drives—a "divine" object for a creaturely or for a perverted object. *Turning* is not a change of objects but a change of basic life movement: it is a swing from being doubled back within oneself (*Rückbiegung*), arranging all things, including God, about oneself as so many objects; it is a swing outward toward the Other (*Hinwendung*), toward the Between, through which God manifests Himself as the Presence in the present (§ 58). Response to the individual Thou's that meet us there is

68. "What Is Common to All," KM, p. 107. Hence the falsity of Helmut Kuhn's claim that Buber "shifted the center of creativity from solitude to community," so that men become creative by "huddling together" (Review of BMM, *Journal of Philosophy*, XLVI [1949], 79).
69. "The Question to the Single One," BMM, pp. 54–55.
70. "What Is to Be Done?" KM, p. 110.
71. WM, BMM, pp. 126, 132, 199.
72. "The Question to the Single One," BMM, p. 55.

like following up various streams which all pour into one Ocean; they all lead to God by virtue of "the one boundless flow of real life." Just as one cannot clearly discern where the streams end and the ocean begins, so, according to Buber, we cannot rigidly determine the exact point at which relation to the finite Thou becomes relation to God.[73] But here one cannot reach the Ocean except by following the streams: saying Thou to the creatures is ultimately saying Thou to God. Hence, far from being freed from the central stream of man's life with man, the religious man is plunged into it more deeply (§ 59).

In a sense this draws him, like Kierkegaard's religious man, beyond the duties and obligations of the ethical man, for he has reached the ground out of which all real norms derive. But unlike Kierkegaard, one is not freed thereby from responsibility for the world. There is a more basic responsibility to the situation where decision must constantly be made anew (§ 59).

Buber here espouses a species of "situation ethics," but it is not an ethics without an absolute principle. The principle is the integrity, i.e., the undividedness, of both the self and the Other, which must be established and preserved in every situation. That, however, is no abstract principle, since its application has to be made anew in each new situation. What is called for is renewed attentiveness to the manifestations of the Thou. Buber will admit that most of traditional moral values are implied in the Thou-relation: one must not lie, kill, or steal, one must honor one's parents, and so forth. Buber will likewise engage frequently in moral condemnations: against the Nazi war crimes,[74] against deceit "under all circumstances," [75] against violence,[76] against seduction,[77] against racial discrimination.[78] "Man

---

73. To say that, however, is by no means to claim that "divinity . . . is the very core of that other person" (Wheelwright, "Buber's Philosophical Anthropology," PMB, p. 85); though God is most intimate to His creatures and speaks through them, He is not their core, for they stand over against Him. Cf. Heidegger's notion that the roots of metaphysics fade off into the soil of Being ("The Way Back," pp. 207–8).

74. "Genuine Dialogue and the Possibilities of Peace," PW, p. 232.

75. *An der Wende*, JSJ, p. 176.

76. "And If Not Now, When?" IW, p. 238.

77. "The Education of Character," BMM, p. 108.

78. "Nationalism," IW, p. 221.

must expound the eternal values." [79] But there is a sense in which these are merely the pragmatic prerequisites for the continued existence of society.[80] Furthermore, in each concrete context it has to be decided anew, for example, what real honoring of one's parents actually means,[81] or even what not killing means, as, for example, in the case of Abraham or in times of war. To serve human fulfillment, these norms all have to be recast again and again in the fire of meeting.[82] The task of human life is not to become "good" but to become "holy," i.e., really related to the transcendent Thou.[83] Hence the essential thing about even the Ten Commandments is not the objective norms but the meeting with God out of which they initially emerge.[84] However, men, with their pragmatic bent, are always intent upon taking out of that meeting something "practical" and something stable upon which they can base their security. Personal *command* (*"Thou* shalt . . ."*) that arises out of the I-Thou situation of the Ten Commandments becomes transformed into impersonal *maxim* (*"One* should . . ."), with universal, objective validity.[85] Men can then perform their "duty" and thus feel themselves "justified" and "moral"; but "there is nothing that can so hide the face of our fellow-men as morality can." [86] Morality has to be grounded ever anew in presence and thus in authentic religiousness.[87]

For Buber the essence of God's revelation is not a new set of object structures but simply fundamental *presence*. It is from that Presence that full human meaningfulness streams into man's world, loosening up the structures that have become rigidified

79. "Replies," PMB, p. 720.
80. "What Are We to Do about the Ten Commandments?" IW, p. 86.
81. "Replies," PMB, pp. 697–700.
82. "The Education of Character," BMM, p. 114.
83. EG, p. 104.
84. "Ten Commandments," IW, pp. 85–88.
85. "The Education of Character," BMM, p. 114.
86. "Dialogue," BMM, p. 18.
87. EG, p. 98. Rotenstreich points out that Buber has here reinvoked the Scholastic notion *Ens et bonum convertuntur* ("Some Problems," p. 153). He is likewise moving toward the original classical notion of prudence. See also Friedman, *Life*, pp. 198–207, and "The Basis of Buber's Ethics," PMB, pp. 171–200.

and depersonalized, introducing new structures, but always in terms of the limitation and necessary modification intro- duced by the age as appropriated by and forming the one who enters into the Presence. Here Buber expressly refers to the Sinai revelation in support of his thesis on the nature of revelation. What God tells Moses is not His name as One Whose essence is to be; rather, according to Buber, He says that "I shall be present as which I shall be present." [88] He is the Thou Who cannot be conjured because He is never absent. He is the One Who is always *there,* always present as the meaning of life. It is a Presence that presents itself with an evidence stronger than the evidence of the senses (§ 60).

Involved here is one of the fundamental problems of philo- sophic thinking, namely, what is the kind of evidence that fur- nishes the point of departure? For positivism it is the publicly verifiable evidence of the senses; for others it is the multileveled evidence presented by the facts of being, perceiving, and think- ing. For Buber all this is conditioned, relative; all this belongs to the realm of objectivity.[89] There is, however, another type of evidence, one not readily accessible but capable of being uncov- ered by one who has become whole and who is open to meeting. But it is likewise a type of evidence that will be readily rejected as sheer gratuity by those who have failed to see it. However, it is accepted with gratitude by those who confront it. What it gives is

88. *Moses, The Revelation and the Covenant* (New York: Harper Torchbooks, 1958), p. 52. Smith's translation here (p. 112) falls into the routine translation of the Genesis text, "I am that I am," which Buber *expressly* rejects (*Moses,* pp. 51–52; EG, p. 62), and which does not faithfully render Buber's German, "Ich bin da als der ich da bin" (W I, p. 154).

89. The thesis that objectivity is relative and conditioned has occasioned the question on the part of some commentators (e.g., Marvin Fox, "Some Problems in Buber's Moral Philosophy," PMB, pp. 151–70) as to the compatibility of this assertion with Buber's moral condemnations. As we have pointed out, Buber replies that there are "eternal values"—but it is their relation to the concrete situation that is shifting and problematic *and relevant to life.* But Buber's preoccu- pation with the latter is so strong that he tends to overstate his case. An adequate account of the situation would have to distinguish enculturated from transcultural elements. Buber's basic distinction between I-Thou and I-It relations is itself a claim at the latter level. See below, pp. 119 ff.

the meaning of one's life.[90] "True revelation reveals to you yourself."[91]

FINALE: REVELATION AND HISTORY (§ 61)

HAVING ROAMED BACK AND FORTH in §§ 52–60 dealing with various aspects of God and the world, the text moves to a close in an orderly presentation which advances by turning about a single theme: the way of God in history. The principle governing the treatment is that God by *His* nature cannot become It: He is the *eternal* Thou, always present, always fulfilled in Himself, whereas creatures are only Thou from time to time and continually lapse again into the condition of It. And yet, because of the way *man* is, God is constantly treated as an It-for-man. The becoming-It-for-man of the God Who in Himself is always Thou Buber treats in two circling lines of exposition: (1) in terms of man's desire for continuity in relation to God[92] and (2) in terms of the being and becoming of the universe as realized in man through the cycles of growth and decline of the Word from Revelation to Form to Object.[93]

The first line of exposition treats of the shift from presence to nonpresence that stems from man's desire for possession. Man wants a God Who is predictable and capable of being handled, One Who gives security. Hence man tends to make God into an It in time and space as a *faith object,* perduring through time and spanning the moments of relation, and as a *cult object,* extended in space through connection with a community of worshipers.[94] Just as every meeting with the forms of the spirit leads to the embodiment of the Thou in the chrysalis of objectification, so meeting with God leads to the embodiment of the forms of meeting within the community. The act of relation is completed in this way by being sent into the world as the source of new meaning in a set of new ways to give a sense of Presence to the whole of man's life. Original faith (Hebrew *emunah*), which moves from the forms to the Presence, is gradually forgotten in favor of the acceptance of a faith object: faith is trans-

90. See "The Faith of Judaism," IW, p. 22.
91. EG, p. 99.
92. Smith, pp. 113–16.
93. *Ibid.*, pp. 116–19.
94. See EG, p. 13; "Symbolic and Sacramental Existence," OMH, pp. 166 ff.

formed into belief (Greek *pistis*) in a dogma.[95] Greek visual thinking supersedes Hebrew aural thinking, and for Buber the dogmas that result are "the most exalted form of invulnerability against revelation." [96]

The system of cult objects and faith objects must be continually penetrated through and through by each member of the community's opening again and again to the Presence, as it opens itself up in the sphere between I and Thou in every life relation. When the whole community opens itself in this way, an authentic mode of human dwelling in the world totality, an authentic human cosmos, emerges. Meeting with God occurs, not only as a summons out of the community, but also as a sending into the community to do the work of God, which is the preparation for the divine indwelling, the preparation of the carriage of God's majesty in the world.[97] God does not remove a man from the world but turns him to it more deeply. Hence there is a rhythm here; meeting and mission, summons and sending, alternate. The authentic man of the spirit receives a summons from above, not for the purpose of being preoccupied with the Above but for the purpose of returning creatively to the community, contributing to the formation of the human cosmos (cf. § 50).

Two dangers stand waiting at this point of the road: For the man of the spirit there is the danger that he may try to dwell in the spirit apart from the world. But God leaves man, or rather man leaves God, when man will not go forth from the meeting; man remains with God only when he goes forth to perform his mission in the world. For the community there is the danger that the forms the creative man introduces become hardened into mere objects, rendered opaque by man's attitude of separation from meeting. Here the transition from religiousness to religion occurs, and for Buber "the primal danger of man is 'religion.' " [98] For, "if there is nothing which can so hide the face of our fellow-man as morality can, religion can hide from us as nothing else can the face of God." [99] Atheism may arise at this point, but

---

95. For Buber the transition is exemplified in the transition from Judaism to Pauline Christianity (*Two Types of Faith,* pp. 43–50).

96. "Dialogue," BMM, p. 18.

97. "The Life of the Hasidim," HMM, pp. 118–19.

98. "Spinoza," OMH, p. 94.

99. "Dialogue," BMM, p. 18.

it is not necessarily a Godless atheism. The so-called atheist may be rejecting an empty set of notions about God and a set of practices that have ceased to refer men to the Presence (cf. § 45). It is then in terms of a greater sensitivity to the mystery of being, which he cannot clearly formulate, that he comes to reject "God" (cf. § 59).

The second line of exposition focuses upon the realization of the two primary metacosmic movements of the universe itself in relation to the eternal Thou (§ 54). The *Urform* of the universe is the polarity between being and becoming. When it reaches the stage of the human being, this tension is expressed in the I-Thou and I-It relations. Through man's turning to relation, grounded upon spirit as relation to the Transcendent, the being of the universe is realized as return to the Source. When this return becomes more explicit, the forms of the spirit appear through creative individuals. Revelation takes on a content which is nothing but the way in which Presence is expressed through the whole being of the creative one, formed by a fusion of his peculiarities with the materials of the age.[100] New form is born upon the earth as more and more provinces of the world are taken over by the spirit to become theophany. The world is set on a new course of becoming, introduced by the adventures of spirit. But at this point belief and cult, which came into being through the development and embodiment of the forms, cause the forms to harden into objects. God becomes an object of faith or else is absorbed into the soul of man in pseudomysticism.[101] A new situation ensues, a new revelation is prepared, which, when it bursts forth, creates a new set of forms out of the material provided by the situation.

The Word appears on earth in revelation; this is the time of renewal, of freshness, of inspiration. It works out its effect in the formation of a cosmos of forms that is penetrated with the power of meeting. But it degenerates when these forms become

100. See "Symbolic and Sacramental Existence," OMH, p. 156, on the *nabi*.

101. Smith's translation of the *Verseelung Gottes* here as "emptying God of soul" is far off the mark. Buber uses the term *Verseelung* elsewhere ("Von der Verseelung der Welt," *Nachlese*, p. 146) with reference to the world and defines it as the *inclusion (Einbeziehung)* of the world in the soul.

"the accepted thing";[102] the cult is "what one does" because "that's the way we've always done it"; the formulas of faith are "what one says," and the Word becomes a set of slogans.[103] And the self who exists within this hardened world of It becomes alienated from true meeting and thus from himself. The material of the age is shifting, preparing for a new revelation.

But history is not simply a matter of the rhythm of the rising and setting of revelation; this cyclic rhythm proceeds in a downward spiral as the world of It becomes more oppressive with the advance of history. We reach the modern world, where even the objective formulations of the divine are called into question. The suprasensible world has disappeared, and God has died. The atheism inherent in the world of It has worked itself out to its logical conclusion.[104] We have reached the age of the eclipse of God.[105] Yet even this is part of the Way, for the alienation, once seen, provokes a turning all the more profound. Out of the experience of dividedness, the drive for unity emerges: a drive for that identity-in-difference through which the eternal Presence shines. This is redemption.

102. *Gültigkeit.* Smith's *currency* is not too helpful.
103. "The Question to the Single One," BMM, p. 43. Again Buber saw Hasidism as the "attempt to rescue the sacramental life of man from the corruption of the facile and familiar" ("Symbolic and Sacramental Existence," OMH, p. 170).
104. *Daniel*, p. 91.
105. EG, pp. 13–24.

6 / The Ontological Foundations: Summary and Conclusion

TOWARD THE END OF HIS LIFE Buber described the character of his work in the following terms:

> I build no towers, I erect bridges; but their columns are not sunk in "isms" and their arches are not fitted together by means of "isms." [1]

But earlier (1923) he said that his position, which maintains the primacy of

> reality grasped as being, in which everything psychological and everything cosmological, everything over-against and all mutual inclusion are embedded, we can, with circumspection, call for the moment *ontologism*—a third position which unites psychologism and cosmologism. But be careful! With qualification! With exact knowledge of the limitation of what is said! What we are discussing is a problem, not an answer.[2]

Buber's fundamental position is an "ism" and yet not an "ism." It is an "ism" because it is a position that stands against other positions; it is not an "ism" because it points to a place and calls for an action, but it claims no exhaustive insight into the ultimates—indeed, it denies that such insight is even possible.

The place it points to is the Between, which is the presence binding together subject and object in every act of awareness. It is neither subjective nor objective. If, *per impossible*, one were to

1. IMB, pp. 84–85.
2. "Von der Verseelung der Welt," *Nachlese,* p. 149. Translation mine.

remove the subjective and objective elements from it, the Between for Buber would still exist as a surplus, for it is the place where the Transcendent is present in the world. It is the place where subjectivism and (for Buber) its projected correlate termed objectivism are transcended by man's reaching *Being,* which encompasses and grounds Buber's *ontology.*

Men develop different modes of dwelling, either with reference to the Between or apart from it, either in an authentic *cosmos* or in an oppressive It-world. These modes of dwelling are the historic world views peculiar to each culture and to each group within a culture; indeed, to a certain extent, they are peculiar also to each individual within the group. Buber attempts to build bridges between men by stressing the relativity of world views within the absoluteness of the Between, which is the place of meeting.

The Between is the place where the I—which is the *conscious* self—and the *manifest* Other arise simultaneously. But both arise as embedded in nature, which is the depth within which the columns of Buber's bridges are actually sunk, and both are held together by reference to the Transcendent, which is actually the keystone holding the arches of each of the bridges together. However, these two—the depths and the heights—are for Buber not comprehensible but only apprehensible. There is no system that can encompass them, for in either case the principle of contradiction does not hold, and it is that principle that grounds the possibility of any system. But there is a reference to the depths and the heights that is awakened through the act of meeting.

What meeting means, Buber describes negatively. In itself, meeting is an encounter of *un*divided with *un*divided, an encounter that is *im*mediate. It presupposes the full presence of both partners and issues forth in a mutuality of effects. Buber shows what the negative characteristics of undividedness and immediacy mean by showing the dividedness and mediation of man's usual reference to things. The self is generally engaged in multiple acts of intending—perceiving, thinking, willing— which have as their objective correlates multiple intended aspects of the Other. But for Buber all such acts involve the mediation of a subjective structure: perceiving views things in terms of the needs of the organism, filtering off from the Other only those aspects that suit biological adjustment; thinking views the unique individual in terms of its reference to a universal framework set up by the mind; and willing views the Other in terms of aims set up by the subject. Willing may hide itself behind the objective truths of thinking, considering itself to be freed thereby of subjectivism; but since, for Buber, thinking itself involves the limitations of the human intellect as a constructive faculty, this is only another mode of subjectivism, all the more insidious because it hides behind "objectivism." Since the Other here is treated, not as it is in itself but in terms of human evaluation, such a position involves an underlying value-nihilism: the valuable-in-itself is not respected. Hence for Buber our usual relation to what meets us is mediated and divided by our own humanly subjective mode of evaluation.

The Between is beyond subjectivism and objectivism—indeed, it is always implicit as their sustaining ground; but it is always in danger of being forgotten. The Between is the *presence*, the immediate, binding and encompassing subject and object. Though the Between comes to be only through man, it is yet that which grounds man as man. The Between is identified as spirit, and spirit in turn is identified as man's relation to that which transcends the world.

The grounds for asserting spirit as relation to the Transcendent seem to lie in the precondition for man's knowing the Other. This involves a relation between knowing the individual and knowing the world, for the individual is always given to man as in the totality and as related to the totality. But to be aware of the totality—and indeed to be aware at all, either of the individual or of the totality or of both—one must be *other* than that of which he is aware. This basic otherness which sets man off from the totality, and thus grounds a view of the totality, Buber terms man's *Urdistanz*, his primal distance. Since reference to the Transcendent provides distance from all immanence, it would seem that we could identify spirit with *Urdistanz*.

But *Urdistanz* is not only distance from the Other; it is likewise distance from the natural givenness of the self. Man has a cosmic-metacosmic origin; he is not only sent from above (as spirit), he is also arisen from below (as nature). The latter is his mode of insertion into the world totality, but the former is the ground for the manifestation of that insertion. Initially these aspects are united in the unconscious, which Buber terms "the undivided primal world which precedes form." Man is no centaur, but man through and through. Immanence and transcendence unite in him in a way which goes beyond the principle of contradiction. Mind-body dualism is only the phenomenal way in which this basic unity can be manifest to man—though it also involves the danger of a split within man's life.

However, not only the world of the individual is involved, but also the world totality. The unconscious is the Great Mother who encompasses the living. To have a soul is to be related to this totality. Each man is a cosmic entity, not in the sense that he is located in the cosmos, but in the sense that his own being extends to the world totality, as the Orientals maintain.[3] In the womb of his mother every man knows the universe. Hence for Buber, at the lower end, so to speak, of the Between, i.e., when we consider man's rootedness in nature, the principle of contradiction does not hold.

Man proceeds out of the world of the unconscious, which is the world continuum. He proceeds out of it through the accentuation of physical distinctness in a complex and centralized body. Through the dawning of spirit in man's *awakening* to his own distinctness, he proceeds toward another form of continuity which is not a reabsorption but the achievement of an identity-in-difference that occurs in the depths, in the Between, which is where man's "innermost" self is developed. The "holy sparks" in things belong to the root of *man's* soul. Because of this insight, Buber will reject experiences of absorption—either ecstatic suspension of the self in God or introspective reduction of all to the self—as subhuman, a reversion to an inferior level of the universe where there is continuity without difference.

This position may appear paradoxical—Buber would say that the principle of contradiction does not hold—because most of our modes of thinking are built up out of our sense perception, which yields distinct, self-contained objects. To be self-contained, to be a unit, at this level of sense perception, is to be *separated* from the others. But if we use as our point of departure, not sensory objectivity, but reflection upon awareness, then we see that to be aware is to *transcend* one's bodily difference in terms of identification with otherness. But such identification with the Other *as other* presupposes a distinctness and hence a

3. "Ueber Jakob Boehme," *Wiener Rundschau,* V (1901), 251–53.

nonidentity; it presupposes a possession of the self as self so that the others can be revealed as *other than oneself*.

Now, once man begins to be aware of his distinctness through the development of his self-consciousness—which need not, and indeed usually does not, involve an explicit awareness of his transcendent reference—he is capable of entering into a more profound relation with the Other *or* of persisting in the distance by contenting himself with the organization of his experience of the Other for his own subjective aims (whether covertly through "objectivity" or overtly through blatant egoism). However, both of these options—entering into more profound relation or persisting in his distance—originate out of primary presence, out of the Between.

It is in that presence that the self and the manifest Other emerge simultaneously. The self emerges as a manifestation of otherness and discovers itself in that very manifestation. To the extent that the Other is allowed to appear *as other,* to that extent is the self constituted as self. Total otherness is revealable when one transcends the subject-object relation in a relation of undivided to undivided which Buber terms the I-Thou relation.

The maturing of the I-Thou relation depends upon a reflective discovery of the I and, following from that, the manifestation of multiple objective aspects with reference to the Other. Reflection upon the I, in turn, takes place in terms of the objectification of self-structures as well as in an immediate reflective self-identification, a presence of oneself to oneself. This furnishes the grounds for a more profound "seeing the other side," a realization of what the Other must be like in its subjectivity. Objectification of the multiple aspects of the Other takes place in terms of either sensory objectification or the more abstract objectification of intellectual construction. Both modes enlarge the Other and ground the *possibility* of a deepening apprehension of the Other.

But the *actuality* of such apprehension becomes increasingly rare, for objectification always constitutes a danger, first, because for Buber it actually consists in viewing the Other in terms of the self, so that it contains the danger of a subtle subjectivism, and second, because the transition from objectification to presence is difficult and unpredictable. One is more apt to leave the place of meeting in favor of the security of the humanly reconstructed world. Real otherness disappears, and with it both the authentic self and the Transcendent, Who speaks only through presence, through meeting with the Other in the Between.

It is only in the I-Thou relation that the Between comes into being as such: spirit appears in the world and fills it with meaning. Presence is deepened. And because of spirit's relation to Transcendence, grounding this relation to otherness, presence to the Other opens up to presence to the Transcendent.

Just as relation to the unconscious and to the world of nature out of which man emerges is shrouded in darkness as the lower level, where for Buber the principle of contradiction does not hold, so also relation to the Transcendent likewise disappears in the clouds above, where the principle of contradiction is likewise suspended. Freedom and dependency in our relation to the Transcendent, and being and becoming, as well as immanence and transcendence in the Transcendent Himself, remain as insoluble antinomies.

That God is transcendent is, for Buber, given in the transcendent reference of man as it comes to fruition in encounter with God as He addresses us through creation. That He is immanent appears in His self-manifestation through His presence in the world through man. That He is being in Himself appears in the revelation of Himself as the eternal Thou Who can never become It. This is the experience of the Presence which is always there, always addressing us, but from which we are continually turning aside. That He is nonetheless involved in becoming is given for Buber in the very fact that He enters into dialogue and hence into relation with the becoming of the universe through man. However, all these claims merely point in a direction rather than constitute knowledge of what God is. Buber claims to speak primarily of man's relation to God; and he claims to speak of God only insofar as He is apprehensible—not comprehensible —through meeting.

The point of meeting with God is to produce the being of the world by turning it to its Source and to assist at its becoming through the creation of new forms. Meeting with God involves mission to the world; summons from God involves sending into the world. In man the cosmos from which he has sprung is brought into the Presence, returned to its Source. It is in man that spirit and nature are joined, and thus full dwelling in Presence, full mutuality, is possible.

Buber speaks of a mutuality of which even a stone is in some sense capable. Nature "says" something to man. And yet, because of the unclarity (and for Buber the unclarifiability) of the relationship between meeting the finite Other and meeting God —the streams all flow into the Ocean—it is not certain whether the things themselves address man or God addresses him through things or both. It may be that their very being is God's address.

It is when one becomes in some way cognizant of that address, when one grasps in some way something absolute and unconditioned, that the forms of the spirit come to birth. But for Buber that takes place only in terms of man's being with other men. The feral man, wild and solitary, is not explicitly aware of the transcendent reference and consequently creates no forms of the spirit. One reason is that the forms appeal to the human community in which they seek embodiment. Hence Buber insists that it is the interhuman realm that is the real bearer of the Between; it is here that whatever man encounters in solitude is "raised to being."

All such encounters with the forms involve a demand for embodiment in the human world. First is the universal demand to form one's own life in terms of openness to the Other; but in certain creative types there is a further demand to create a special new form on earth: a new work of art, a new set of conceptual relations, a new social form. But the highest form-creation of all is the creation of man's life in *explicit* reference to the Transcendent Thou. This is the work of the religious creator, as particularly embodied in Jesus.

All such forms are both conditioned by, and in turn help to form, the common world of men. They are conditioned by the common world because it is the common world that forms the man in his way of thinking and seeing, in his fundamental mode of presence—all of which varies from culture to culture and from epoch to epoch. But the forms also pour back into the common world to make transparent to the age the spirit which originally appeared on earth in the forms of the past.

As long as such a world remains open to the Transcendent through each individual's again and again responding to the

Thou, dwelling in nearness to nature, to the works of the spirit as embodied and as calling for embodiment, but, above all, dwelling in nearness to other individuals, such a world is uplifting. A living time and a living space are maintained, qualitatively articulated in terms of the mutual interchange especially operative in the holy places and on the holy days. But when these structures no longer are rendered transparent through man's open attunement, activated ever anew, they become oppressive.

This is true of all human worlds. But as history advances, the objective structures become more tightly woven, terminating in a conception of universal causal determinism operative within the framework of abstract space and time. Living space and living time gradually give way to clock time and mathematically measured space: a system of qualitatively undifferentiated points within which all entities can be located. And the entities themselves are broken up into equivalent elements found in each, combined and separated according to necessary laws. The holy has disappeared.

But it is part of the Way of God in history to disappear, for His absence provokes a stronger yearning for His Presence. The way is being prepared for a more profound revelation out of which new forms will emerge upon the earth. The place they appear is the Between, and they appear only through the fundamental act of man's being, whereby he comes to dwell in presence.

Buber's lifelong preoccupation has been with the problem of unity in multiplicity. His final synthesis is one in which he gathers into a unity the multiple polarities he had noted earlier: spirit and matter, matter and form, being and becoming, reason and will, positivity and negativity.[4] He accomplished this by introducing his own polarity, I-Thou and I-It, and then developing its implications in a way which integrates the traditional polarities.

I-Thou accomplishes the turning of the universe to *Being*: in the I-Thou relation man produces the being of the universe through turning it to its Source. This occurs in the Between, which is *spirit* as relation to the transcendent Source which gives

4. See above, p. 16.

a fullness and *positivity* to life. Spirit, in turn, is united indissolubly to *matter* to form the human totality. Out of the I-Thou relation, developed in explicit reference to something bearing an absolute character, the *forms* of the spirit emerge and transform the already formed *material* on hand in the age and available to the creative one. This adds to the *becoming* of the universe within which the I-It relation emerges. *Reason* finds its place here as a contribution to the becoming of the world in the I-It relation. But this results in a gradual alienation of man from the Thou and thus from the Absolute. When this occurs, man's world is gradually drained of meaning. But the *negative* experience of absence provokes a profound yearning for fullness and positivity: the *will* to enter into relation is awakened. Man turns again to the Source through relation to the Thou, and the whole process is set in motion again.

We have seen how this second great Copernican revolution in modern thought both assimilates and reverses the first such revolution. At the level of objectivity, Kant is correct: objects are structured by the knower, for whom they supply the material. But at the ontological level, the self who knows (and desires and feels and senses, etc.) is basically relation to the Other in itself. The Other as existent, in its unfathomable depths, has absolute primacy over the Other as object. To that extent, Buber returns to the medieval tradition that moved (with significant variations) through Aquinas to Scotus and Occam as to the primacy of existence, haecceity, and singularity, respectively. Yet Buber carries forward that earlier tradition in an important way: he articulates the way in which the existent is accessible and the way in which relation to the existent opens up to relation to God. A purely theoretical existentialism which asserts the primacy of existence quite often gives the impression of merely doing that —asserting it—and then it goes on juggling with concepts! Buber's existentialism is one in which concept formation is a means, not merely for a set of correct judgments about reality, but, more basically, for a more profound *dwelling* face to face with the existent. To that extent, to be, for Buber, is to be more profoundly present to the Other.

This gives further specification to the Neoplatonically inspired thesis that the being of an entity is its *lumen* (Plotinus,

Dionysius, Aquinas).[5] But *lumen* here is to be understood not basically as the capacity to reveal oneself to another or as an ability to grasp universal, essential structures; it is rather an ability to stand in the presence of reality, to let the Other be present in its otherness to the self. Hence we have a way of putting into its fuller human perspective an intellectualism which tends to see human superiority as a matter of a superior capacity to grasp universal, essential principles. From Buber's point of view, such a capacity is merely a superior ability to contribute to the *becoming* of the world-for-man. But the contribution to the *being* of the world is through that fundamental mode of superiority which is the capacity to dwell more deeply in the presence. That means that the absolutely superior man is the one who really loves.

God Himself is total Presence without absence, the Source of all light, i.e., the Source of all being. Man as the *imago Dei* is the ability to be more deeply present. This ability is itself grounded upon man's own a priori reference to the Transcendent, so that he who learns to dwell in the presence of beings is the one who actualizes his own personal reference to God.

An integral existentialism would not only have to assimilate these insights; it would likewise have to develop a more adequate doctrine of essence and objectivity than Buber develops. Buber's conceptual relativism is a justifiable reaction against a tendency —all too common—toward absolutizing concepts at a certain level. Yet Buber insists that there is an essential distinction between I-Thou and I-It, no matter what terms are used to express it. He further distinguishes two different modes of space, time, and causality: one a set of human constructs brilliantly analyzed by Kant and especially operative in science—and these belong to the I-It domain; the other a set of lived categories of mutual interrelation, spatiality, and temporality growing out of authentic encounter. Here Buber is moving back toward the earlier notions developed prior to the rise of modern science. He also speaks of certain eternal truths in the realm of ethics. But his center of attention is fixed upon the application of the "eternal verities" to the flux of the concrete situation, which is replete with novelties. To that extent, he is moving toward the classical

5. Thomas Aquinas, *Supra librum De Causis expositio,* lectio 6 (Parma edition, Vol. XII, p. 729b).

notion of prudence; but he always tends to overstate his case, and consequently he develops an epistemology which relativizes all objective truth claims. This creates an unresolved conflict with his own claims to nonrelative truths in ethics, in ontology, and in man's original stance toward the world. In spite of itself, Buber's thought bears witness to the fact that there are essential distinctions in reality, and we have access to them in a mode of reflection which is neither I-It, in the totally relativized sense of the term, nor I-Thou. In spite of the enculturated character of most of our human thinking, there are a number of transcultural elements implied in that very recognition.

Like Heidegger, Buber is attempting to get back to the *ground* of metaphysics; and he sees metaphysics itself as often standing in the way of such access. Heidegger wants to get back to fundamental ontology, pondering the "nearness of the near." [6] Thus also Buber: Indeed, he claims to have no metaphysics, to feel neither need for one nor ability to provide one.[7] But he does claim an *ontology*. Metaphysics for Buber seems to imply statements about the transexperiential that often get in the way of our penetrating the experiential. Ontology for him is basically *description* of what is deepest in our experience. Both Heidegger and Buber are fighting the natural gravity which tends to draw metaphysical systems into a static equilibrium where they circle back into themselves and are no longer open to the newly emergent, the historical, situation.

The distinction between ontology and metaphysics here is thus not at all identical with the distinction that appears in Wolff and in Neo-Scholasticism, where ontology deals with the most general principles of being while metaphysics is concerned with the existential questions of God, the soul, and so forth.[8] Nor is it equivalent to the parallel distinction in Sartre's thought, where ontology deals with the general features of reality-in-general while metaphysics deals with the question of the individual processes that lie at the origin of this particular concrete

6. Martin Heidegger, *Ueber den Humanismus* (Frankfort a.M.: Klostermann, 1947), p. 37; see also, by the same author, "The Way Back," pp. 207–21.

7. IMB, p. 84. See above, p. xii, n. 7.

8. For an excellent brief historical survey of the notions "metaphysics" and "ontology" see Joseph Owens, *An Elementary Christian Metaphysics* (Milwaukee: Bruce, 1963), pp. 1–13.

totality.[9] For Buber, metaphysics has to do with the transexperiential, for which he has little use; ontology in Buber's sense points in the direction of the Between and calls for the action of really meeting the Other.

This Between, this relation of the *conscious* I to the *manifest* Other, this open sphere of light, is the place of Being and hence the locus of Buber's ontology. Though his descriptions deal with this locus, the concepts he uses to describe it are not part of a self-contained system; rather, they are indicators of transconceptual reality. They point to the place and call for an action: the action of really learning to *meet* the Other. Here and here alone is Being to be found as the real "object" of his ontology, and not in any conceptual system.

However, our options are not a closed system or a nonsystematic description. As we have indicated, the recognition of the distinction between I-Thou and a wholly relativized I-It is, on Buber's own admission, an absolute distinction. And the structure of that recognition and of that distinction, in turn, has implications, both antecedent, as to foundations, and consequent. A disciplined attention to those elements should lead us toward a metaphysics whose very structures point to an attention to the historical, to the emergent, but which remain as the transhistorical foundations of historical existence, as stable indicators pointing us in the direction of changing experience. The existential coloration will vary from epoch to epoch—indeed, from person to person—depending upon the context within which such a metaphysics is developed. Or, to change the metaphor, the metaphysical organism will exhibit different features, depending upon its changing relationship to its environment; but there will be structural principles governing the total process and the transition from one condition to another. "Process," "condition," "transition," and the recognition of such notion-in-general, as exhibited by particular contexts, lead us back to all the traditional problems designated as "metaphysical": the problems of Being and our knowledge thereof.

Thus there are two things about "metaphysics" that seem to trouble experientially descriptive thinkers like Buber: (1) a (well-grounded) hesitancy with regard to assertions about the

9. *Being and Nothingness*, trans. Hazel Barnes (New York: Philosophical Library, 1956), p. 619.

transphysical, about that which is not in some way exhibited "in the earth of bodily meetings" but which, it is sometimes claimed, inhabits a "heaven of abstractions," [10] and (2) a justifiable reaction against the notion, generally associated with metaphysics, of a "system" as a closed totality claiming adequate knowledge of ultimates.

However, with Buber's own experiential descriptions (his "ontology") as a basis, it should be possible to develop a metaphysics grounded in the dialectical structure of incarnate spirituality, which is man himself. Such a metaphysics would be rooted, on the one hand, in presence to individuals as revealed in and through our bodily meetings and, on the other hand, in a reference to the fullness of Transcendent Being grounding the peculiarity of our individual encounters. Such a transcendent reference would constitute the absolute horizon revealed only as the not yet possessed term toward which all our positive illuminations direct us—revealed, therefore, as the Absolute Mystery. It should then be possible to press beyond Buber to the cosmic depths and the transcendent heights where, according to Buber, the principle of contradiction, necessary for all systematization, does not hold. We should be able to do this by developing an analogous understanding of the notion of Being and thus of the principle of identity (whose negative expression is the principle of contradiction). To be is to be complete self-identity in that unique instance of the Eternal Thou Who in His nature can never become It. But as absolute mystery, such self-identity can only be affirmed, never fathomed by limited being. In the case of inner-worldly beings, self-identity is in dialectical tension with lack of self-identity owing to the negativity involved in incarnate existence: sprung from what was not itself, dependent upon what is not itself, changing into what it is not yet, and projected toward a term when it will no longer be. From chaos to man, incarnate existence is in a progressively heightened tension between self-identity and its negation. But from chaos to the Eternal Thou, self-identity is analogously realized.

Developing these lines of thought, we could possibly achieve, not only an ontology in Buber's sense of a description of encounter with Being, but a metaphysics in the sense of a grasp of what is implied but not directly experienced in that ontology. But we

10. IMB, p. 57.

will have to turn elsewhere for further development along these lines.[11] Buber is dead. The fuller implications of his thoughtful experience remain to be carried out.

11. For a preliminary sketch of such a metaphysics cf. Robert E. Wood, "The Self and the Other: Towards a Reinterpretation of the Transcendentals," *Philosophy Today*, X (spring, 1966), 48–63. For a detailed grounding of certain fundamental features of this metaphysics cf. Karl Rahner, *Spirit in the World*, trans. William Dych (New York: Herder & Herder, 1968), especially Part III, "The Possibility of Metaphysics on the Basis of the Imagination," pp. 387–408.

BIBLIOGRAPHY

I. Primary Sources

A. German Texts

"Antwort." In *Martin Buber*. Edited by Maurice Friedman and Paul Schilpp. The Library of Living Philosophers. Stuttgart: Kohlhammer, 1963.

Begegnung, Autobiographische Fragmente. Stuttgart: Kohlhammer, 1960.

Hinweise. Zurich: Manesse, 1953.

> This volume contains essays from *Ereignisse und Bewegungen* (1914) along with other isolated essays from the period 1909–53.

"Ueber Jakob Boehme." *Wiener Rundschau*, V, No. 12 (1901), 251–53.

Der Jude und seine Judentum. Cologne: Melzer, 1963.

> Along with isolated essays written between 1936 and 1960, this volume contains essays from the following collections:
>
> 1. *Reden über das Judentum* (1911–23). From these essays we have cited:
>   a. "Das Judentum und die Juden"
>   b. "Das Judentum und die Menschheit"
>   c. "Die Erneuerung des Judentums"
>   d. "Der Geist des Orients und das Judentum"
> 2. *Die Jüdische Bewegung* (Vol. I, 1916; Vol. II, 1920). From these essays we have cited:

   a. "Renaissance und Bewegung"
   b. "Das Gestaltende"
3. *Kampf um Israel* (1921–32)
4. *Die Stunde und die Erkenntnis* (1933–35)
5. *Israel und Palästina* (1950)
6. *An der Wende* (1952)

Nachlese. Heidelberg: Lambert Schneider, 1965.

This volume contains a collection of significant essays written between 1906 and 1964 that were not gathered up in the other collections. From these essays we have cited the following:

1. "Gemeinschaft und Umwelt"
2. "Zur Situation der Philosophie"
3. "Von der Verseelung der Welt"
4. "Das Unbewusste"
5. "Nachwort"
6. "Philosophische und religiöse Weltanschauung"

Die Rede, die Lehre, das Lied. Leipzig: Insel, 1917.

This volume contains Buber's contributions to the following anthologies: *Ekstatische Confessionen* (1909), *Chinesische Geister- und Liebesgeschichten* (1911), and *Kalewala* (1914).

Werke. Vol. I, *Schriften zur Philosophie.* Munich: Kösel, 1962.

This volume contains:

1. *Daniel* (1913)
2. *Ich und Du* (1923)
3. *Zwiesprache* (1930)
4. *Die Frage an den Einzelnen* (1936)
5. *Reden über Erziehung* (1926–39)
6. *Das Problem des Menschens* (1943)
7. *Zur Geschichte des dialogischen Prinzips* (1954)
8. *Beiträge zu einer philosophischen Anthropologie* (1962), which contains:
   a. "Urdistanz und Beziehung" (1950)
   b. "Der Mensch und sein Gebild" (1955)
   c. "Das Wort, das gesprochen wird" (1960)
   d. "Dem Gemeinschaftlichen folgen" (1956)
   e. "Schuld und Schuldgefühle" (1957)
9. "Elemente des Zwischenmenschlichen" (1954)
10. *Gottesfinsternis* (1953). A collection of essays from the period 1932–51, originally appearing as a collection in the English translation *Eclipse of God* (1952).
11. *Bilder von Gut und Böse* (1952)

12. *Zwei Glaubensweisen* (1950)
13. Essays from *Hinweise*
14. "Aus einer philosophischen Rechenschaft" (1962)
15. *Pfade in Utopia* (1950)

Werke. Vol. II, *Schriften zur Bibel.* Munich: Kösel, 1963.

Along with a number of short essays from the period 1929–63, this volume contains the following books:

1. *Moses* (1948; Hebrew original, 1945)
2. *Der Glaube der Propheten* (1950; Dutch original, 1940)
3. *Königtum Gottes* (1932; enlarged 1936 and 1956)
4. *Das Gesalbte* (1964; a collection from the period 1938–51)
5. *Die Schrift und ihre Verdeutschung* (1936; enlarged edition, 1962)

Werke. Vol. III, *Schriften zum Chassidismus.* Munich: Kösel, 1963.

Along with a number of shorter essays written between 1906 and 1963, this volume contains the following books and articles:

1. "Die jüdische Mystik," from *Die Geschichte des Rabbi Nachman* (1906)
2. *Die Erzählungen der Chassidim* (1949)
3. *Die chassidische Botschaft* (1952)
4. *Rabbi Nachman von Bratzlaw* (1906)
5. *Gog und Magog* (1949; Hebrew original, 1943)
6. Essays collected and translated into English in *Hasidism and Modern Man*
7. "Zur Darstellung des Chassidismus" (1963)

B. *English Texts*

Between Man and Man. Translated by Ronald Gregor Smith. Boston: Beacon Press, 1961.

This volume contains the following essays:

1. "Dialogue" (1929)
2. "The Question to the Single One" (1936)
3. "Education" (1926)
4. "The Education of Character" (1939)
5. "What Is Man?" (1938)

"Correspondence with Martin Buber," Robert C. Smith, correspondent. *Review of Existential Psychoanalysis and Psychiatry,* VI, No. 3 (1966), 246–49.

Daniel: Dialogues on Realization. Translated by Maurice Friedman. New York: McGraw-Hill, 1965.

Eclipse of God. Translated by Maurice Friedman *et al.* New York: Harper Torchbooks, 1957.

Good and Evil. Translated by Ronald Gregor Smith. New York: Scribner's, 1953.

Hasidism and Modern Man. Edited and translated by Maurice Friedman. New York: Harper Torchbooks, 1958.

This volume contains the following essays:

1. "Hasidism and Modern Man" (1957)
2. "My Way to Hasidism" (1918)
3. "The Life of the Hasidim" (1908)
4. "The Way of Man, According to the Teachings of Hasidism" (1948)
5. "The Baal-Shem-Tov's Instruction in Intercourse with God" (1928)
6. "Love of God and Love of Neighbor" (1943)

I and Thou. Translated by Ronald Gregor Smith. 2d ed. New York: Scribner's, 1958.

Buber's "Postscript" is added to this edition.

"Interrogation of Martin Buber," conducted by Maurice Friedman. In *Philosophical Interrogations*, edited by Beatrice and Sydney Rome, pp. 13–117. New York: Holt, Rinehart & Winston, 1964.

Israel and the World. Translated by Maurice Friedman *et al.* New York: Schocken Books, 1963.

This volume contains essays on Judaism written between 1921 and 1958. From these we have cited the following:

1. "The Faith of Judaism" (1928)
2. "What Are We to Do about the Ten Commandments?" (1929)
3. "Plato and Isaiah" (1938)
4. "Teaching and Deed" (1934)
5. "The Power of the Spirit" (1934)
6. "The Gods of the Nations and God" (1941)
7. "Nationalism" (1921)
8. "And If Not Now, When?" (1932)
9. "Israel and the Command of the Spirit" (1958)

The Knowledge of Man. Edited and translated by Maurice Friedman. New York: Harper Torchbooks, 1960.

This volume contains the following essays:

1. "Distance and Relation"
2. "Elements of the Interhuman"
3. "What Is Common to All"
4. "The Word That Is Spoken"
5. "Guilt and Guilt Feelings"
6. "Man and His Image Work"
7. "Dialogue between Martin Buber and Carl R. Rogers"

Moses, the Revelation and the Covenant. New York: Harper Torchbooks, 1958.

The Origin and Meaning of Hasidism. Edited and translated by Maurice Friedman. New York: Harper Torchbooks, 1960.

This volume contains the following essays:

1. "The Beginnings" (1940–43)
2. "The Foundation Stone" (1940–43)
3. "Spinoza, Sabbatai Zvi, and the Baal-Shem" (1927)
4. "Spirit and Body of the Hasidic Movement" (1921)
5. "Symbolic and Sacramental Existence" (1934)
6. "God and the Soul" (1940–43)
7. "Redemption" (1940–43)
8. "The Place of Hasidism in the History of Religion" (1940–43)
9. "Christ, Hasidism, Gnosis" (1954)

Paths in Utopia. Translated by R. F. C. Hull. Boston: Beacon Press, 1960.

Pointing the Way. Translated by Maurice Friedman. New York: Harper Torchbooks, 1963.

This volume contains essays which appeared in the collections *Hinweise* and *Ereignisse und Bewegungen.* From these we have cited the following:

1. "Productivity and Existence" (1914)
2. "Brother Body" (1914)
3. "With a Monist" (1914)
4. "The Teaching of the Tao" (1909)
5. "Bergson's Concept of Intuition" (1943)
6. "Healing through Meeting" (1951)
7. "Education and World-View" (1935)
8. "What Is to Be Done?" (1919)
9. "China and Us" (1928)

10. "Society and State" (1951)
11. "The Validity and Limitation of the Political Principle" (1953)
12. "Hope for This Hour" (1952)
13. "Genuine Dialogue and the Possibilities of Peace" (1953)

"Replies to My Critics." In *The Philosophy of Martin Buber*, edited by Maurice Friedman and Paul Schilpp. The Library of Living Philosophers. La Salle, Ill.: Open Court, 1967.

Two Types of Faith. Translated by Norman Goldhawk. New York: Harper Torchbooks, 1961.

II. SECONDARY SOURCES

A. *Books*

Agus, Jacob. *Modern Philosophies of Judaism.* New York: Behrmans, 1941.

Anzenbacher, Arno. *Die Philosophie Martin Bubers.* Vienna: Schendl, 1965.

Aquinas, Thomas. *Supra librum De Causis expositio.* Vol. XII of *Opera Omnia*, Parma edition.

Baillie, John. *Our Knowledge of God.* New York: Scribner's, 1939.

Bergson, Henri. *Time and Free Will.* Translated by F. L. Pogson. London: Allen & Unwin, 1950.

Bonaventure. *In Hexaemeron.* Vol. IX of the Peltier edition.

Brown, James. *Kierkegaard, Heidegger, Buber and Barth.* New York: Collier, 1962.

Coates, J. B. *The Crisis of the Human Person.* London: Longmans, Green, 1949.

Cohen, Arthur. *Martin Buber.* London: Bowes & Bowes, 1957.

Cullberg, John. *Das Du und die Wirklichkeit.* Uppsala Universitets Årsskrift, Vol. I. Uppsala: Lundeqvistska, 1933.

Diamond, Malcolm. *Martin Buber, Jewish Existentialist.* New York: Oxford, 1960.

Dilthey, Wilhelm. *Dilthey's Philosophy of Existence.* Edited and translated by William Kluback and Martin Weinbaum. London: Vision Press, 1957.

Feuerbach, Ludwig. *Grundsätze der Philosophie der Zukunft.* Leipzig, 1847.

Friedman, Maurice. *Martin Buber, The Life of Dialogue.* New York: Harper Torchbooks, 1955.

————— and Schilpp, Paul (eds.). *The Philosophy of Martin Buber.* The Library of Living Philosophers. LaSalle, Ill.: Open Court,

1967. (Contributions to this volume are listed by individual authors under "Articles," below.)

Goldstein, Walter. *Die Botschaft Martin Bubers.* 3 vols. Jerusalem: Dr. Peter Freund, 1952–56.

Heidegger, Martin, *Ueber den Humanismus.* Frankfort a.M.: Klostermann, 1947.

Heim, Karl. *Christian Faith and Natural Science.* Translated by N. H. Smith. New York: Harper Torchbooks, 1953.

Joel, K. (ed.). *Aus unbekannten Schriften: Festgabe für Martin Buber.* Berlin: Lambert Schneider, 1928.

Kant, Immanuel. *Critique of Pure Reason.* Translated by N. K. Smith. London: St. Martin's Press, 1933.

Kohn, Hans. *Living in a World Revolution.* New York: Cardinal Pocket Books, 1965.

———. *Martin Buber: Sein Werk und seine Zeit.* 2d ed. With a "Nachwort" by Robert Weltsch. Cologne: Melzer, 1961.

Lang, Bernhard. *Martin Buber und das dialogische Leben.* Bern: H. Lang & Cie, 1963.

Maringer, Simon. *Martin Bubers Metaphysik der Dialogik in Zusammenhang neuerer philosophischer Strömungen.* Cologne: Steiner, 1936.

Michel, Wilhelm. *Das Leiden am Ich.* Bremen: Carl Schünemann, 1930.

Nigg, Walter. *Martin Bubers Weg in unserer Zeit.* Bern: Paul Haupt, 1940.

Oldham, J. H. *Real Life Is Meeting.* New York: Macmillan, 1947.

Owens, Joseph. *An Elementary Christian Metaphysics.* Milwaukee: Bruce, 1963.

Paul, Leslie. *The Meaning of Human Existence.* New York: Lippincott, 1950.

Pfuetze, Paul. *Self, Society, Existence.* New York: Harper Torchbooks, 1954.

Rahner, Karl. *Spirit in the World.* Translated by William Dych. New York: Herder & Herder, 1968.

Sartre, Jean-Paul. *Being and Nothingness.* Translated by Hazel Barnes. New York: Philosophical Library, 1956.

Smith, Ronald Gregor. *Martin Buber.* Makers of Contemporary Theology Series. Richmond, Va.: John Knox Press, 1967.

B. *Articles*

Anzenbacher, Arno. "Thomismus und Ich-Du Philosophie." *Freiburger Zeitschrift für Philosophie und Theologie,* XII, No. 2-3 (1965), 161–90.

Bergman, Hugo. "Martin Buber and Mysticism." In *The Philosophy of Martin Buber*, edited by Friedman and Schilpp, pp. 297–308.

Biser, Eugen. "Martin Buber." *Philosophy Today*, VII, No. 2 (1963), 100–114.

Blau, Joseph. "Martin Buber's Religious Philosophy: A Review Article." *Review of Religion*, XIII (1948), 48–64.

Cassirer, Ernst. " 'Spirit' and 'Life' in Contemporary Philosophy." In *The Philosophy of Ernst Cassirer*, edited by Paul Schilpp, pp. 857–80. The Library of Living Philosophers. Menasha, Wis.: Banta, 1949.

Cohen, Arthur. Review of *The Eclipse of God. Judaism*, II, No. 3 (1953), 280–83.

Fackenheim, Emil. "Martin Buber's Concept of Revelation." In *The Philosophy of Martin Buber*, edited by Friedman and Schilpp, pp. 273–96.

———. "Some Recent Works on and by Martin Buber." *Religious Education*, LIV (1959), 413–17.

Fischoff, Ephraim. Introduction to Martin Buber's *Paths in Utopia*, pp. ix–xxv.

Fox, Marvin. "Some Problems in Buber's Moral Philosophy." In *The Philosophy of Martin Buber*, edited by Friedman and Schilpp, pp. 151–70.

Frankenstein, Carl. "Du und Nicht-Ich: Zu Martin Bubers Theorie des Dialogs." *Stimmen der Zeit*, CLXXVIII, No. 11 (1966), 356–70.

Friedman, Maurice. "The Basis of Buber's Ethics." In *The Philosophy of Martin Buber*, edited by Friedman and Schilpp, pp. 171–200.

———. "Dialogue and the 'Essential We': The Basis of Values in the Philosophy of Martin Buber." *American Journal of Psychoanalysis*, XX, No. 1 (1960), 26–34.

———. "The Existential Man: Buber." In *The Educated Man*, edited by Paul Nash *et al.*, pp. 363–88. New York: John Wiley, 1965.

———. Introduction to Martin Buber's *Daniel*, pp. 3–44.

———. Introduction to Martin Buber's *The Knowledge of Man*, pp. 11–58.

———. "Revelation and Law in the Thought of Martin Buber." *Judaism*, III, No. 1 (1954), 9–19.

Gotshalk, Robert. "Buber's Conception of Responsibility." *Journal of Existentialism*, VI, No. 21 (1965), 1–8.

Gumbiner, J. Review of *Between Man and Man. Commentary*, V (May, 1948), 482–83.

Hartshorne, Charles. "Martin Buber's Metaphysics." In *The Philosophy of Martin Buber*, edited by Friedman and Schilpp, pp. 49–68.

——— and Reese, William. "Martin Buber." In *Philosophers Speak of God*, pp. 302–6. Chicago: University of Chicago Press, 1953.

Heidegger, Martin. "The Way Back into the Ground of Metaphysics." In *Existentialism from Dostoevsky to Sartre,* edited by Walter Kaufmann, pp. 207–21. Cleveland: Meridian, 1956.

Heim, Karl. "Ontologie und Kirche." *Zeitschrift für Theologie und Kirche,* XI (1930), 325–38.

Herberg, Will. Editor's Introduction to *The Writings of Martin Buber.* New York: Meridian Books, 1956.

Husserl, Edmund. "The Crisis of European Humanity and Philosophy." In *The Search for Being,* edited and translated by Jean Wilde and William Kimmel, pp. 378–413. New York: Noonday, 1962.

Kaplan, Mordecai. "Buber's Evaluation of Philosophic Thought and Religious Tradition." In *The Philosophy of Martin Buber,* edited by Friedman and Schilpp, pp. 249–72.

———. "Martin Buber: Theologian, Philosopher, and Prophet." *The Reconstructionist,* XVII (May, 1952), 7–10.

Kaufmann, Felix. "Martin Buber's Philosophy of Religion." In *The Philosophy of Martin Buber,* edited by Friedman and Schilpp, pp. 201–34.

Kaufmann, Walter. "Martin Buber's Religious Significance." In *The Philosophy of Martin Buber,* edited by Friedman and Schilpp, pp. 665–88.

Kuhn, Helmut. "Dialogue in Expectation." In *The Philosophy of Martin Buber,* edited by Friedman and Schilpp, pp. 639–64.

———. Review of *Between Man and Man. Journal of Philosophy,* XLVI (1949), 75–79.

Landmann, Michael. "Martin Buber—Deuter in der Krise der Gegenwart." *Universitas,* XXI, No. 6 (1966), 591–98.

Levinas, Emmanuel. "Martin Buber and the Theory of Knowledge." In *The Philosophy of Martin Buber,* edited by Friedman and Schilpp, pp. 133–50.

Marcel, Gabriel. "I and Thou." In *The Philosophy of Martin Buber,* edited by Friedman and Schilpp, pp. 41–48.

Przywara, Erich. "Judentum und Christentum." *Stimmen der Zeit,* CX (1925–26), 81–99.

Rosenzweig, Franz. "Zu einer Stelle aus Martin Bubers Dissertation." In *Kleinere Schriften,* pp. 240–44. Berlin: Schocken, 1937.

Rotenstreich, Nathan. "Some Problems in Buber's Dialogical Philosophy." *Philosophy Today,* III, No. 3 (1959), 151–67.

———. "Buber's Dialogical Philosophy: The Historical Dimension." *Philosophy Today,* III, No. 3 (1959), 168–75.

Schneider, Herbert. "The Historical Significance of Buber's Philosophy." In *The Philosophy of Martin Buber,* edited by Friedman and Schilpp, pp. 469–74.

Schulweis, Harold. "Martin Buber: An Interview." *The Reconstructionist,* XVII (March, 1952), 7–10.

Simmel, Georg. "The Fundamental Problems of Philosophy." In *The Search for Being,* edited and translated by Jean Wilde and William Kimmel, pp. 315–43. New York: Noonday, 1962.

Smith, Constance. "The Single One and the Other." *Hibbert Journal,* XLVI (1948), 315–21.

Theunissen, Michael. "Bubers negative Ontologie des Zwischen." *Philosophisches Jahrbuch,* LXXI, No. 2 (1964), 319–30.

Von Hammerstein, Franz. "Martin Bubers messianische Hoffnung and ihr Verhältnis zu seiner Philosophie." *Judaica* (Zurich), X, No. 2 (1954), 65–104.

Wahl, Jean. "Martin Buber and the Philosophies of Existence." In *The Philosophy of Martin Buber,* edited by Friedman and Schilpp, pp. 475–510.

Weltsch, Robert. "Buber's Political Philosophy." In *The Philosophy of Martin Buber,* edited by Friedman and Schilpp, pp. 435–50.

———. "Einleitung" to *Der Jude und sein Judentum,* pp. xii–xl.

———. "Nachwort." In Hans Kohn, *Martin Buber,* pp. 413–79.

Wheelwright, Philip. "Buber's Philosophical Anthropology." In *The Philosophy of Martin Buber,* edited by Friedman and Schilpp, pp. 69–96.

Wood, Robert E. "The Self and the Other: Towards a Reinterpretation of the Transcendentals." *Philosophy Today,* X (1966), 48–63.

Index